Copyright © 2021 by Henry Churney
All rights reserved
No part of this book may be reproduced or transmitted in any form or by any means, electronic or mechanical, including photocopying, recording, or by any information storage and retrieval system, without permission in writing from the author.

WITH ALL JEW RESPECT

A book on Jewish Stand-Up Comedians – From Marx (Groucho, not Karl) to Seinfeld

By Henry Churniavsky

CHAPTERS

Chapter 1. Forward by Henry Churniavsky: A story from the Ukraine/Russia to Liverpool.

Chapter 2. What is Comedy Stand-Up? – How did it all start in the USA and the UK?

Chapter 3. The Borscht Belt in the Catskill Mountains of America.

Chapter 4. Pre Groucho Marx – 1867 – 1886: Weber & Fields/Smith & Dale/Ed Wynn

Chapter 5. The Stand-Up Comedians

Chapter 6. Tips for Stand-Up Comedians

The Stand-Up Comedians

1890 – 1977	Groucho Marx
1892 – 1964	Eddie Cantor
1893 – 1980	Lou Holtz
1893 – 1977	Issy Bonn
1894 – 1974	Jack Benny
1896 – 1996	George Burns
1896 – 1968	Bud Flannagan
1898 – 1981	George Jessel
1901 – 1965	Al Ritz (The Ritz Bros)
1902 – 1971	Joe E. Lewis
1902 – 1986	Myron Cohen
1904 – 1985	Jimmy Ritz (The Ritz Bros)
1906 – 2001	Brother Theodore
1906 – 1998	Henry Youngman
1906 – 1997	Sally Marr
1907 – 1986	Harry Ritz (The Ritz Bros)
1908 – 2002	Milton Berle
1908 – 1996	Morey Amsterdam
1909 – 1985	Mickey Katz
1909 – 2000	Victor Borge
1910 – 1973	Jack E. Leonard
1911 – 1971	Belle Barth
1911 – 1974	Harvey Stone
1911 – 1980	Samuel Levenson
1911 – 1985	Phil Silvers
1911 – 1987	Danny Kaye
1911 – 2010	Jean Carroll
1914 – 1982	Joe E. Ross
1916 – 2006	Jan Murray
1918 – 2007	Joey Bishop
1919 – 2006	Red Buttons

1921 – 2004	Rodney Dangerfield
1922 – 2015	Jack Carter
1922 – 2014	Sid Caesar
1922 – 2020	Carl Reiner
1923 – 1987	Dick Shawn
1923 -	Larry Storch
1924 – 2003	Buddy Hackett
1924 – 1973	Allan Sherman
1924 – 1999	Gary Moreton
1924 – 1987	Jackie Vernon
1925 – 1966	Lenny Bruce
1925 – 1980	Peter Sellers
1925 – 2017	Shelley Berman
1925 – 1990	Sammy Davies Jr
1926 – 2017	Don Rickles
1926 -	Shecky Greene
1926 – 2013	Mike Winters
1930 – 1991	Bernie Winters
1926 – 2017	Jerry Lewis
1926 -	Mel Brooks
1927 – 2004	Alan King
1927 – 2021	Mort Sahl
1927 – 2018	Will Jordan
1927 – 2020	Jerry Stiller
1927 – 2020	Norm Crosby
1928 – 1982	Bette Walker
1928 – 2021	Jackie Mason
1930 – 1978	Totie Fields
1931 – 2014	Mike Nichols
1932 -	Elaine May
1933 – 2014	Joan Rivers
1934 – 1982	Marty Feldman
1935 -	Woody Allen

1936 – 2014	David Brenner
1936 -	Arnold Brown
1937 -	Freddie Roman
1942 -	Robert Klein
1943 – 2019	Freddie Starr
1944 – 2014	Harold Ramis
1944 -	Richard Belzer
1945 -	Gabe Kaplan
1946 – 1989	Gilda Radner
1947 -	Larry David
1947 -	Albert Brooks
1947 -	Richard Lewis
1948 -	Lewis Black
1948 -	Billy Crystal
1949 – 1984	Andy Kaufman
1949 – 2016	Gary Shandling
1950 – 2010	Robert Schimmel
1951 -	Yakov Smirnoff
1952 -	Elaine Boosler
1952 -	Alexei Sayle
1952 -	Roseanne Barr
1953 -	Ruby Wax
1953 -	Rita Rudner
1954 -	Jerry Seinfeld

This book is dedicated to my beloved wife, Vivien and my twins: Natalie and Sam

I would also like to thank a number of other people who have helped me in my life:

My dad, **Ralph,** who was my inspiration for getting into comedy.
My mum, **Sheila**, for giving me life and the material for solo shows!
My sisters, **Gail and Lorraine**, who said that they would not get a mention!
My cousins, **Karen and Franklyn** - he pushed me to do this book.
Craig Fox, for taking my daughter off my hands.
Angus Matheson, my photographer – for the front and back cover.
Adam Carr, for pre-reading and a helping hand.

Thank you also to comedy legends:

Sam Avery, his comedy course, started all this for me.
John Wilson, who got me to carry on and is now a close friend (yep, it's his fault!)
John Prosser, for suggesting the title for this book and my show.

Profits from the sale of this book are going to 'Laugh For Life', a charity for Mental Health awareness for young people.

Chapter 1 - Henry Churniavsky. Where did I come from?

'One is not truly dead until one's name is forgotten.'
Unknown.

Actually, maybe my name should be - Henry Sapozhnikpof Churniavsky!

Where did I come from? What I mean is where did the 'Churniavsky' & 'Sapozhnikpof' names come from?

I am lucky that my Churniavsky family have been able to go back and find our roots, our origins.

Thank you to all my family, especially Rochelle Cooke, who put so much of our family history together and to Franklyn Churney, my cousin, who said I should add this to my book.

It starts, I suppose, with Golda Chernyavsky (there are so many ways this name has been spelt by our family). Golda, born in 1773, married Mendel Chernyavsky (her second marriage) and gave birth to a son Geinakh (Genckh) Mendeliovich Chernyavsky in 1806. Genckh also married twice, the second time to Khaya Yudkova (born 1806). They had five children. One of them was Shmuel Mordecai Churniavsky, who in turn had four children. One of these children, Henoch *(who I am named after)*, was my great grandfather. Henoch was married to Nechumah *(Hannah – who unfortunately passed away 20 days after my birth)*. They had six children: Hetty, Harry (my grandfather), Louis, Barney, Tevy and Bessie.

Harry married Edna Buckley, and they had two children; Ralph *(my father)* and my Auntie Arline *(who I was very close to)*.

My father, Ralph, married my mother, Sheila Lewis (Sapoznikpof), who had three children. I am the eldest *(thank G-d for that)*, and my two sisters, Gail and Lorraine.

So, then it's me. Henry Churney (Churniavsky), I was fortunate to marry Vivien Specter, and we had twins on the 29th June 1988 – Natalie and Samuel.

So that's the family tree on one side *(there are 100s of us)*. But where did it start with Golda?

It starts in the Ukraine with Henoch, who was one of four siblings (brothers Abram and Nachum, and sister Khaya Rachel). The brothers eventually emigrated to Britain to start new lives.

The Chernyavskys, it is believed, were living in the Belaya Tserka area in a shtetl (a small town) named Tarascha. Tarascha is about 150km south of Kiev. In 1765, there were only 134 Jewish residents there. By the end of the 19th century, this had increased to 4,905, which made up 44% of the population.

It is thought that at some time, part of the family moved (Henoch and Nachum, definitely) to Kremenchuk before they took the trip to Britain.

Kremenchuk is approximately 200km from Kiev, next to the River Dnieper. In 1897, the Jewish population was 29,876, which was about 40% of the total population. Jews were not allowed many jobs at the time, and most made a living from tailoring.

My father told me of a story in the 1800s when the three brothers (Henoch, Abram & Nachum) were in their youth; soldiers would come to the shtetl and force Jewish boys into the Russian army. Nachum and Abram were hidden for a time by a non-Jewish family. The family were called Pearlman (or Pearlstone), and for a time, the brothers took the name of the family who helped them.

The three brothers eventually made it to Liverpool. The Immigration Office had difficulty in translating the surname, so it seems two brothers were called Shenofsky (later Shaw), and my great-grandfather was called Churniavsky (later Churney). They all settled in Liverpool as cabinet makers.

On my mum's side, our roots again go back to Kiev, Ukraine, with David Leib Shepoznikopf (a bootmaker), who also emigrated to Liverpool and was given the name Lewis as part of the integration process when, believe it or not, immigration, on their arrival, could not understand their name! So they put down Lewis.

David was one of six children to Joseph Sapozhikopf (my great-great-grandfather). David, as I have stated, was a bootmaker; he also had a hobby - having children. Thirteen in total, with two wives (*Not at the same time!*). Nine by his first wife Sarah, who bore Nathan (my grandfather was the sixth child) and four to Hannah. It took some of the brothers and sisters over 20 years to meet due to a number of factors. Some of the family decided to leave Liverpool and move to America. My grandfather stayed in Liverpool and became a tailor; he even made suits for Ken Dodd (*and I think he was paid in cash for that*). My grandfather lived in what is now China Town, Nelson Street. Bizarre, when I was about six or seven years old, my father used to take us to a Chinese restaurant in China Town, that this restaurant frequently visited for 30 years, turned out, in fact, to be the house where my grandfather was raised.

I was going to perform under the name Henry Shepoznikopf Churniavsky but decided against it for two reasons. One, can you imagine an MC introducing me?

And secondly, I priced up the cost of my name on t-shirts – they were out of the question; it was ridiculous.

So there you have it. I settled on Churniavsky, my stage name, as it is very important to me. My father never got the chance to see me perform my comedy, so I decided after he passed away that I would continue the old family name as a tribute to him for getting me into comedy and also as a tribute to the rest of my family.

Chapter 2 - What is Comedy Stand-Up?

Stand-up is a comic style in which a comedian performs in front of a live audience, usually talking to them and trying to make them laugh! *(Well, as a stand-up comedian myself, performing as Henry Churniavsky, sometimes I don't get any laughs, but that's another story).*

Being a comedian or comic is to use stories, jokes, one-liners, monologues - anything to entertain a crowd and get a reaction. Some comedians will use props, music, or even tricks to entertain.

America – Stand-up

Humour/comedy goes back a long way; it's even mentioned in the Bible! The Hebrew word 'Yitzhak' means laughter.

In America, comedy started with Minstrel shows in the early 19th century. It also had roots in various traditions of popular entertainment of the late 19th century, i.e. vaudeville, music halls, early variety shows, and humorous monologues from authors like Mark Twain.

When Jews moved to the USA in the 19th century, they brought with them their own history of humour which is the basis for a lot of comedy today.

Jews loved the self-mocking humour. It was Lenny Bruce that said, 'The Jewish religion was not just a religion but a state of mind, a condition, a way of looking at the world.' Maybe that's how we as a Jewish community have survived.

At the end of the 19th century and early 20th century, America received a large number of Jewish immigrants. They had to work hard to survive, as nothing was given to them. An escape from all the hardship was in the form of 'The Yiddish Theatre' in New York and in similar venues in other major American cities. It was how vaudeville was born; acts would come along, be themselves, speak Yiddish, and entertain the crowds.

Vaudeville grew all over the States, with a range of acts such as magicians, musicals, acrobats, and, of course, comics. Many of the early performers were just children; it was their escape. In fact, many of the early, great comedians cut their teeth in the harsh world of vaudeville. Eddie Cantor once said, 'I pranced around the stage, singing and telling jokes to avoid being hit by rotten produce.'

The Yiddish Theatre seemed to fade in the 1920s as vaudeville became more popular. It was in the theatre that comedians would tell jokes in Yiddish and add a few English words to their set. Comedy teams seemed to be popular at this time, such as Weber and Fields, Smith and Dale.

At the turn of the 20th century, American humour began to change. The comedians of this time often depended on many different forms of comedy, including fast-paced joke delivery, slapstick, lewd innuendo, and different ethnic mixes such as African, Scottish, German, Jewish. Many of these acts based their routines on popular stereotypes.

The Founders of Modern America are where we find many of the Jewish comics starting to come into stand-up. The Founders are the names given to stand-up comedians who came from the Vaudeville or the 'Chillin Circuit' that spoke directly to an audience. It was also a collection of performance venues throughout the Eastern, Southern and Upper Mid-West areas of America, including such names as Jack Benny, George Burns, Milton Berle, along with the likes of Frank Kay, Moms Mabley, Bob Hope, and Fred Allen. It was around this time Jewish comedians began to go to the Catskill Mountains in New York, especially in the summer holidays, to entertain the Jewish families who holidayed there and wanted to be entertained in the evenings. This area was also known as the 'Borscht Belt'. It was there that many vaudeville acts would try their luck, but many were lost in the transition; costumes and Yiddish accents were seen as old hat. It was a new era of comedy and Jewish comedy. Audiences, now second-generation, English speaking Americans, wanted more. The Borscht Belt resorts were now run by entertainment people, seen as social directors. They were known as 'Tummlers' (A Yiddish word for fun makers). These guys had to make sure the acts were good and that they could cater for all audiences at the resorts. *(Now that is a job and a half)*. Many comics cut their teeth this way - Jerry Lewis, Milton Berle, Danny Kaye, Phil Silvers.

Vaudeville was dying towards the end of the 1920s; movies started to take over, and the vaudeville theatres were transformed into movie theatres.

In the 1930s and 1940s, many entertainers used radio, and from the 1950s, television. In the 1940s, a Jewish entrepreneur (and gangster, it was reputed), Benjamin 'Bugsy' Seigel, transformed Las Vegas and made it a gambling and entertainment centre. Still, he would only hire the best singers and comics, such as Joey Bishop, Rodney Dangerfield, Jackie Mason and Don Rickles.

Now nightclubs and resorts have become a breeding ground for stand-up comedians such as Joan Rivers, Lenny Bruce, Woody Allen, Shelly Berman, and many others.

In the 1950s and the 1960s, folk clubs were a base for even more comics, such as Mort Sahl and others. Comedians from San Francisco and New York were bringing in social satire and started to push the boundaries of stand-up by including politics, race, and sex in their sets. Lenny Bruce, before he came to the UK, was regularly arrested for using obscene language. George Carlin was also arrested in the early 1970s.

The 1970s saw some stand-up comedians become major stars, e.g. Richard Pryor and George Carlin. Stand-up started to expand from clubs to major arenas; Steve Martin and Bill Cosby had different styles to many others. Older comics like Rodney Dangerfield, Buddy Hackett and Don Rickles enjoyed a revival late in life. Television, with the help of programs like 'Saturday Night Live' and 'The Tonight Show', helped to progress stars like Bill Maher and Jay Leno.

The 1970s to the 1990s saw different styles of comedy emerge. We had madcap with Robin Williams, observation with Jerry Seinfeld, the ironic comedy of Steven Wright, and other comics like Eddie Murphy, Ellen DeGeneres, Whoopi Goldberg. These were major stars who would go on to influence many of the comedians we see today.

United Kingdom – Stand-up

Stand-up comedy began in the United Kingdom in the music halls of the 18th and 19th centuries. But it was in the 20th century via the variety theatre circuit that it really took off, with the likes of Morecambe & Wise, Arthur Askey, Max Miller, Issy Bonn, and Ken Dodd. But until 1968, comedy was heavily censored by the Lord Chamberlain's office, which required that all comedians had to submit their acts for censorship. The act would then get their submissions back with sections in blue, which were deemed inappropriate. Acts like Mike and Bernie Winters, Arnold Brown, and Peter Sellers also grew from this era.

In the 1960s, we saw the satire boom, which opened up another genre, which included the arrival of the club The Establishment, which opened up spots for even more comics. It brought to the UK acts from America, including Lenny Bruce.

By the 1970s, music hall entertainment was ending due to the rise of television and radio. Working men's clubs had now evolved, which brought to prominence such comics as Bernard Manning, Frank Carson, Stan Boardman, and many others, who also made it onto Television. Another avenue was the folk club scene, where we see artists like Billy Connolly *(my ultimate comedy hero),* Mike Harding, and Jasper Carrot cut their teeth on stand-up.

In the late 1970s, London saw the opening of American style stand-up clubs like the Comedy Store, which was opened by Peter Rosengard and Don Ward. This was the start for alternative comedy stars in the 1980s, such as Dawn French, Jennifer Saunders, Alexei Sayle, Rik Mayall, and Ade Edmondson, to name but a few.

In the 1980s and 1990s, we saw numerous comics entertaining us, and Freddie Starr was amongst many who grew in popularity.

My Book:

In this book, I want to look at the Jewish contribution to stand-up comedy from both America and the United Kingdom. My look at these stars will include some of their famous quotes for you to read and enjoy. I've added some personal thoughts into the mix and some of my stand-up material. Please indulge me in my new passion; I hope you enjoy it and spread the word.

I'll start in America and add the UK comics as I go along.

The first comedian may not have been your standard stand-up comic, but I do feel he is relevant *(well, he's Jewish for a start, so that helps!),* and it is from a personal perspective that I have included him *(I will explain later in the book).*

But before we get into the comedians themselves, let me tell you more about where many American Jewish comedians cut their teeth in their quest for fame and fortune.

Chapter 3 - The Borscht Belt in the Catskill Mountains of America

Borscht Belt *(The word comes from borscht, a soup of Ukrainian/ Russian origin, made with beetroot)*. This is a term for Jewish summer resorts in the Catskill Mountains that were popular vacation spots for many Jewish families from the 1920s through to the 1960s *(remember the film 'Dirty Dancing'?)*. It started the culture for 'Alrightniks' *(a Yiddish term for all right-people)* and 'Balbatish' *(respectable/well mannered)*. These were Jewish people- single, couples or families who wanted a holiday away from work.

Borscht Belt hotels, summer camps, and *kuchalayns* (*a Yiddish name for self-catered houses*) were frequented by middle and working-class Jewish New Yorkers, mostly Ashkenazi Jewish immigrants from Central and Eastern Europe and their children and grandchildren, particularly in the 1940s, 1950s, and 1960s. Because of this, this area was also nicknamed the Jewish Alps.

This was the start for many of the bigger names in comedy, including Woody Allen, Rodney Dangerfield, Milton Berle, Jackie Mason, Lenny Bruce and Mel Brooks, to name but a few. It was also a breeding ground not just for comedians but also for other artistes and talented people who were discovered by many consumers. They also became household names in music, acting, television, the stage, playwriting, directing and producing and whose work has lasted for generations.

The Borscht Belt started when farmers in the area opened their doors to 'city folk' in the summer to supplement their earnings. The entertainment side was a bit extra, but really, they knew nothing about show business, and they resented having to pay for musicians and entertainers. However, as the years went on and more people with an eye for business and profit got involved, this evolved into a mega business for lots of owners and stars. At its peak, the Borscht Belt would house five hundred hotels and three thousand bungalows. As the hotels grew and competition between them grew, they needed to bring in bigger and more famous artists. At one point in time, on a Saturday night, you could find Sammy Davis Jr., Jerry Lewis, Sam Levenson, Lou Holtz, Eddie Fisher, Julie Garland, Tony Martin and the Ritz Brothers all playing in different venues in the Catskills.

At the beginning of the Borscht Belt, the main entertainer was a man who would be referred to as a Toomler *(Tummler)*. It was his job to perform all sorts of roles and to entertain the guests of the summer resort. He would have to be able to sing, act, be the camp clown, and at times, MC. He would also write, direct and produce shows for everyone. The Tummler could be working 18-hour days as he was the official noisemaker, the fun-generator and organiser. For this, the most he would earn was $20 a week plus his keep and lodgings. By the 60s, when the big talent agencies became involved, entertainers could be earning $1,500 - $2,000 a night.

There were hundreds of other comics/singers who originated in the Borscht Belt/Catskill Mountains, who made some impact on the Jewish history of comedy; too many to mention, but here are a few names of some of these comedians with short biographies:

Al Kelly (Abraham Kalish) **(1896 – 1966)** – born in Russia, a vaudeville comedian, known for his double talk act. He mainly performed in the Borscht Belt.

Gene Baylos (1906 – 2005) – a nightclub comedian. He was a favourite of the 'celebrity' comedians in New York. Performed on 'The Hollywood Palace', 'The Joey Bishop Show', 'The Dick Van Dyke Show' and 'Car 54, where are you?'. Starting in the Catskills in the 30s, he then worked the nightclub circuit from New York to Los Angeles. He accused Jerry Lewis of stealing his style; "He stole my body. I asked Dean (Martin) to tell him to stop, and he didn't. I didn't talk to Dean for five years."

For 30 years, every morning, he left his home to go to the Friars Club. He would, on the way home, buy food for the homeless. One day a friend of his offered a homeless man some clothes, to which Baylos said, "Get your own bum." On stage, he would rush on as if he was late, "I've just returned from the dentist." As he was praising the dentist's work, white bits would fall out of his mouth.

B.S. Pully (Murray Lerman) **(1910 – 1972)** – A New York nightclub comedian and stage actor, famous for the role of Big Jule in 'Guys and Dolls', he was famed for his 'blue' material and thick tone.

Joey Adams (Joseph Abramowitz) **(1911 – 1999)** – was an American comedian, vaudevillian, radio host, nightclub performer and author who wrote about the Borscht Belt in 1973 (*thank you, Joey, for much of the information; The Borscht Belt by Joey Adams with Henry Tobias*). Born in New York, he wrote a column in the New York Post called 'Strictly for Laughs'. With a career spanning 70 years, he performed on the radio and wrote books about humour. He is cited to be the first to say, 'With friends like that, who needs enemies?'

Phil Foster (1913 – 1985) – An American actor who was best known for his role in the TV sitcom 'Laverne & Shirley'. He made his debut in the late 30s and made a name for himself in the Catskills.

Jackie Miles (1913 – 1968) – Born in Russia. An actor and comedian. A stand-up comedian who was on the Radio Hall of fame. Made several records including 'J.Schwartz',' New York' and '120 Pounds Dripping Wet'. A sad-faced comedian who used a Yiddish accent for his comedy.

He was once talking about his first trip to Florida. "I found a beach. No one was on the beach. So, I put my towel down and went into the ocean. When I came out, a big man with a Southern accent said to me. 'What are you doing here? Didn't you see the sign? It says, Private Beach. No Swimming Allowed.' I said to him, 'Oy. To me, the sign said: Private Beach? No! Swimming Allowed.'"

Larry Best (1917 – 1985) – New York. Comedy actor – 'The Bellboy' (1960) – LP – 'Color Me Jewish' – comedy set to music.

Jackie Wakefield (1924 – 2010) – A Borscht Belt comedian and singer for over 50 years. He toured with Sammy Davies Jr. and Engelbert Humperdink. He appeared on Broadway 1955, in 'Catch a Star' and 1964 'I had a Ball.' He appeared in over 1,000 commercials.

Mal Z. Lawrence (1937 – 2021) – actor-writer, Album 'Mal Z. Lawrence.'
Broadway shows 'Straight Jacket' & 'Borscht Belt Buffett'. He has performed for 30 years in Las Vegas and Atlantic City.

Larry Alpert (1949 – 1996) was in; Yiddish musical 'Bagels and Yox' Broadway 1951 and 'A Tree Grows in Brooklyn.' Comedian and actor. 1961 – Broadway 'Let It Ride'.

Lee Tully – a Chicago born comedian who found fame in the 40s in the Catskills. After discovering heartburn, he wrote his first hit, 'Essen', a big Yiddish hit. He performed 'Kosher Comedy' with songs like 'Oomglick Blues' and 'Litvak and Galitz' all on his first album 'Selzer on the Rocks.'

Dick Capri (Richard Crupi) – born in Pennsylvania. His style, using his Italian heritage and unique delivery mix of comedy and mime, was started in the Borscht Belt. He has played every major medium, nightclubs, arenas, TV and Broadway. He also has performed for two USA presidents, Gerald Ford and George Bush.

Jackie Kannon (1921 – 1974) – Jackie was a nightclub comedian born in Windsor, Ontario. Son of a Rabbi. He found fame with an act in his 'Rat Fink Club' in the 60s.

Stories from the Borscht Belt

When **Phil Silvers** came to the Catskills to work at Saltz's Hotel in 1931, he was an established burlesque comic. He demanded $500 for the summer. His sketches alone were worth the money, but to earn such a salary, Phil also had to play the clarinet in the brass section.

Everyone has heard of **George Burns**. However, starting out in the Catskills at The Lakeside Inn, its owners Messrs Fish and Stein only wanted at the time a certain Sid Gary, who was big in vaudeville. His act developed into a double act called Burns and Gary. His first partner was none other than George Burns, who, as you will read later on went on to be one of the biggest entertainers in America.

Henny Youngman was a Toomler in the early days. Youngman played the violin only because his mother insisted he had music lessons at an early age. He was, in 1932, performing at The Swan Lake Inn. His violin playing was part of his comedic act, but one day the Social Director was ill and did not show up; Youngman, a man who had been thrown out of Manual Training High School for clowning, found himself stepping out of the band and into the spotlight as a comedian. From that day, he never looked back. His famous lines included.
'Now take my boss - please'. 'He's got borscht instead of blood in his veins. He's the biggest man in 'Who owes who.'
'There is something about him that his creditors like, but he won't spend it.'
'I get plenty of exercise; every time he gives me a check, I have to race him to the bank.'
'When it comes to money, you've got to hand it to him; he'll get it anyway.'
'But I can tell he wants me around. He keeps giving me post-dated checks.'

The title 'King of the Catskills' has to be awarded to **Danny Kaye.** In 1933 his first job was as part of the entertainment staff at the White Roe Lake. He was 20 and was learning the job the hard way - one play a week and a different variety show every night. He also had to entertain the residents at breakfast, lunch and dinner- his only time to rehearse was late into the night. Danny had a lot to thank the Catskills for when he became a movie star in the future. It was because of his time in the Catskills that he was able to travel with the Abe Lyman Orchestra to Japan, China and Siam as a dancer in 1934 and perform gigs in Greenwich Village in New York. The boy worked hard. His fortune changed when he met Max Liebman; Max recognised the talent before him and got him cast in the Yiddish version of The Mikado. Danny, as well as owing his public success to the Catskills, was also grateful to the Catskills for his personal happiness, as this is where he met Sylvia who he married in 1940.

George Jessel started out performing at the Roxy. A routine/ monologue called 'Mamma on the telephone' was picked up by others and used elsewhere in the Catskills, and it included such classic lines as:

'Hello, Mama? This is your son, Georgie – yeah, from the checks every week. How do you feel? Do you still get those dizzy spells?... You get them every five minutes? And they last a half hour! Why don't you call Dr Wolf? You've lost confidence in him? Oh, when he gets sick, he calls in another doctor!'

'Mamma, how do you like the love bird I brought for the front room? You cooked it? You cooked a South American bird? A bird that speaks three languages? Oh, you didn't know. He should have said something!'

This type of act was used by many different comics, including **Shelly Berman** and Bob Newhart. The mother sketch is still used today in different forms; **Nichols & May** did a great double act on this subject. Jewish comics love to do stuff on their mothers (*hey, I've done a whole show on mine!*).

Sam Levison remembers the Catskills with fondness; "I don't think I did much for the mountains, but they did plenty for me. They took me out of the tenements for several summers, provided me with tuition for college and much good subject matter for my unanticipated career in comedy. Let's give the little hills a big hand."

Red Buttons started in the Catskills at Beerkill Lodge. He had four roles - entertainer, bellboy, prop boy and waiter. As he was an apprentice Borscht Belter, he made a dollar and a half a week, but he was clever at making money on the side.

Sid Caesar eventually became a big star, as with Danny Kaye, thanks to meeting Max Liebman. It was thanks to meeting Max Liebman that he won the Broadway role in 'Tars and Spars'. Sid started as a sax player in the Avon Hotel. It was here he fell in love with the owner's niece, Florence. The owner Meyer Arkin was not impressed with the attention that Sid was giving Florence. Sid used his influence and asked for a spot as a comedian. It worked; he got laughs. However, the laughs it is said went to his head, and he approached Arkin and asked for two dollars a week more in his salary. Arkin was not best pleased and refused. Sid insisted that as his future nephew-in-law, he was worth more than the $10 he was getting as a sax player. He told him he was doing more and deserved due consideration. Meyer agreed, said he was a reasonable man and told him he would be more considerate, and he didn't have to play with the band at lunch-time. In 1939 he married Florence and was still performing at the Vacation Hotel, and despite having a rich backer, he was still doing both roles for $12. In 1941 he started as a full-time comic at Kutscher's Country Club for $100 a night.

Around 1940 a new talent was emerging, **Buddy Hackett.** He remembers the time when the hotel owner was paying Buddy's father $13 for 13 hours as an upholsterer, and he added a dollar on for Buddy. Buddy remembered for many years later that same owner wanted to book Buddy to play. Buddy now was getting $500 a night, and he told the owner he would not take the booking until he received $600 plus $12. It paid him and his father many years back pay.

Buddy was 16 when, due to a comic not turning up, he was offered $5 to perform. It was, in his words, a disaster, so much so he thought the audience was going to kill him. He finished that season as a waiter.

Buddy loved to get attention. On the next Memorial Day, he rammed his car into the Swan Hotel porch just to get attention. On the 4th of July, he put dry cereal into the dining room fan and was seen laughing at the resulting indoor snowstorm when the maître d' turned on the fan.

Another famous American started his career at a very young age in the Catskills. Danny Levitch (Lewis) was a Jolson-type singer, and his mama Rae was a piano player. Every summer, Danny would wait for the call that booked him for the summer at the Catskills. As part of any deal, his son, **Jerry Levitch (Lewis),** was included. At 14, Jerry was a tearoom boy at Brown's. Even at this young age, Jerry would play for laughs, dropping trays of peach melbas or falling into mash potato just to raise smiles from everyone. At 15, he pushed and pushed his father to get him a spot for the Labor Day show. A spot was eventually given to him, and as the story goes, his parents were too nervous to attend, and they did not want to put a young Jerry off his stride, but they would know by the tone in his voice how well he had done. Danny decided to ring Jerry but to disguise his voice and pretend to be a booker to offer Jerry a job. The conversation went something like this:
"Hello, is this Jerry Lewis. This is Al Rock, the agent. I liked your act tonight and would like to use you on some of my dates."
"Gee, thanks a lot, mister," Jerry reacted excitedly. "But how can you like my act? I haven't been on yet." The rest, as it is said, is history.
There were, of course, casualties in the Catskills. Some acts failed to make the grade, and some made mistakes

but did go on to make a big name for themselves. Two, in particular, were **Jackie Mason** and **Alan King.**

Jackie Mason started out under the name of Jacob Masler. His first Catskill job was at Sunrise Manor. He appeared on stage, and his first words were, "This place stinks." Well, these were his last words as the boss went backstage and threw him out. This did not put him off, nor owners from booking him, but it is reported that he, especially as an MC (Master of Ceremonies), got what is called 'spotlight-hogging.' At the Pioneer Hotel, he was booked for a season as MC. He could not help himself. Sometimes he would take half an hour to introduce the guest act. He even at times borrowed the guest's own material. On one occasion before bringing on Phil Foster, Jackie took 45 minutes of Phil's act. When Phil finally came onto the stage, he said, "How, do you do, ladies and gentlemen. You just heard my act, so good night," and walked off stage and out of the hotel.

When **Alan King** started at the Catskills, he thought he would not last the first weekend. He was a drummer in a band, but to show his versatility, he would ride on a horse with Indian feathers and fall off; he would also throw himself into the pool just to get a laugh. At 15, he got his first job to try-out for the Decoration Day weekend. He got his chance at the Hotel Gradus with the opening line, "When you work for the Gradus, you work for gratis!". Overnight, he was out of a job.

Below I have set out some of the jokes used by many mentioned in my book. It's amazing that there were no swear words!

"I just got back from a pleasure trip. I took my mother-in-law to the airport."

"I've been in love with the same woman for 49 years! If my wife ever finds out, she'll kill me!"

'What are three words a woman never wants to hear when she's making love? "Honey, I'm home!"'

"Someone stole all my credit cards; I'm not reporting it. The thief spends less than my wife did."

"We always hold hands. If I let go, she shops."

"My wife and I went back to the hotel where we spent our wedding night; only this time I stayed in the bathroom and cried."

"My wife and I went to a hotel where we got a waterbed. My wife called it the Dead Sea."

"She was at the beauty shop for two hours. That was only for the estimate. She got a mudpack and looked great for two days. Then the mud fell off."

"The Doctor gave a man six months to live. The man couldn't pay his bill, so the doctor gave him another six months."

Doctor called Mrs Cohen saying, 'Mrs Cohen, your cheque came back.' Mrs Cohen answered, 'So did my arthritis!'

Doctor: "You'll live to be 60!"
Patient: "I am 60!"
Doctor: "See! What did I tell you?"
Patient: "I have a ringing in my ears."…
Doctor: "Don't answer!"

A drunk was in front of a judge. The judge says, "You've been brought here for drinking."
The drunk says, "Okay, let's get started."

Q: Why do Jewish divorces cost so much? A: They're worth it.

Q: Why don't Jewish mothers drink? A: Alcohol interferes with their suffering.

Q: Why do Jewish mothers make great parole officers? A: They never let anyone finish a sentence!

Q: How many Jewish mothers does it take to change a light bulb?
A: Don't bother. I'll sit in the dark. I don't want to be a nuisance to anybody.

Chapter 4 - Pre Groucho 1867 – 1886

Weber and Fields: An American comedy team known as Mike & Meyer on stage were popular at the turn of the 20th century. Joe Weber (Joseph Weber) 1876-1942 & Lew Fields (Lewis Maurice Fields) – 1867-1941. The duo was known for its slapstick sketches in what was called a 'Dutch' dialect. They first appeared in The Bowery in New York at only nine years old. They went on to perform in San Francisco, where they appeared for ten weeks, earning them $250 per week.

In 1885 they formed their own company and 20 years later took over the Broadway Music Hall. Their musical shows 'Twirly Whirly', 'The Geezer', 'Whoop-dee-Doo' and 'Hoity Toity' consisted of songs, comedy, and burlesques. Despite the success, Fields left to open his own theatre in New York. They both still performed as solo artists until 1912, when they reunited to produce 'Hokey-Pokey' at the Broadway Music Hall. Weber continued as a solo act until 1927, and Fields until 1930. In 1932 they again reunited for the inaugural show at the Radio City Music Hall and were also seen on the movie 'Lillian Russell', performing their 'casino' routine.

Their comedy routines included 'The Pool Man', 'The Horse Race' and 'The Schutzenfest', all between 1892 – 1995.

It is said that Neil Simon's play and film 'The Sunshine Boys' is based on Weber and Fields.

Weber & Field's Famous lines as Mike and Myer:

Mike: 'I am delightfulness to meet you.'
Myer: 'Der disgust is all mine.'
Mike: 'I receividid a letter from mein goil, but I don't know how to writtenin her back.
Myer: Writtenin her back! Such an education you got it? Writtenin her back! You mean rottenin her back. How can you answer her ven you don't know how to write?'
Mike: 'Dot makes no, never mind. She don't know how to read.'

Smith and Dale: Joe Smith (Born Joseph Seltzer 1884-1981) & Charlie Dale (Born Charles Marks 1885-1971) were a famous American vaudeville comedy duo who grew up in New York. Meeting as teenagers in 1898, they decided to perform as a duo.

In 1902 they joined up with two singing comedians. They formed 'The Avon Comedy Four' and, despite changes in the line-up, became a successful comedy act in vaudeville, and for over 15 years, they were top performers on Broadway. By 1919 The Avon Comedy Four had broken up, and Smith and Dale continued their act on Broadway and vaudeville, which included the Palace Theatre. Both used a heavy Jewish accent, with one speaking very deep while the other in a high pitch.

The 1920s saw them at the height of their success with the sketch 'Doctor Kronkheit and his only living patient'.

Several films followed in the late 1920s (known as the talkie boom). In 1932 the film 'The Heart of New York' showcased Smith and Dale's act in a feature movie with the pair playing professional matchmakers, who were constantly arguing with each other. They also appeared in 'Two Tickets to Broadway' (1951).

They continued to work together well into their late 80s and appeared on stage, radio and TV, and were frequent guests on New York's 'Cavalcade of Stars' and 'The Steve Allen Show'.

Smith and Dale's Famous lines:

Smith: 'Are you a doctor?'
Dale: 'I'm a doctor.'
Smith: 'I'm dubious.'
Dale: 'I'm glad to know you, Mr Dubious.'

Smith: 'Look at this, Doctor!'
Dale: 'Look at ...oh, that there? Did you ever have that before?'
Smith: 'Yes, I did.'
Dale: 'Well, you got it again.'

Smith: 'Doctor, it hurts when I do *this..*'
Dale: 'Don't *do* that!'

Ed Wynn 1886 – 1966

Wynn, born Isaiah Edwin Leopold, was born in Philadelphia. An American actor and comedian. He was known for his 'Perfect Fool' comedy character.

Starting his career in 1903 in vaudeville, he was also part of the 'Ziegfeld Follies' in 1914.

Radio dominated the early 1930s for Wynn, but he insisted on playing to a live audience. In 1936 Wynn did a brief ad-libbed spot, on Television, during an NBC broadcast. Wynn hosted the first comedy-variety television shows on CBS.

In 1959 Wynn switched from comedy to become a serious actor. His performance in 'The Diary of Anne Frank' in 1959 earned Wynn an Academy Award nomination for best supporting actor.

Wynn's voice was used in Disney's 'Alice in Wonderland', playing the Mad Hatter. He also was part of the team in 1965's 'That Darn Cat'.

Even to the end, Wynn was comical. His bronze grave marker reads 'Dear Gd: Thanks...Ed Wynn.'

Ed's Famous Quotes:

'A bachelor is a man who never makes the same mistake once.'

'I've found a formula for avoiding theses exaggerated fears of age; you take care of every day - let the calendar take care of the years.'

'Every radish I ever pulled up seemed to have a mortgage attached to it.'

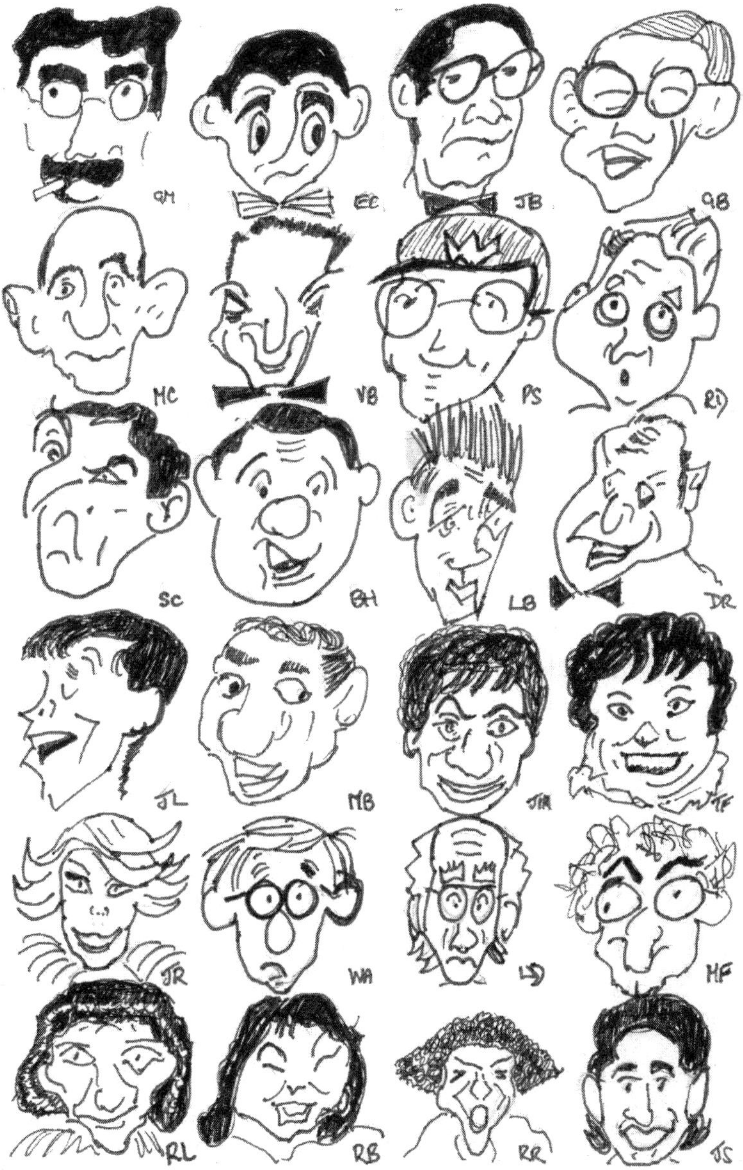
EC
JB
MC
VB
PS
SC
BH
LB
DR
JL
MB
JM
TF
JR
WA
MF
RL
RB
RR
JS

Chapter 5 - The Stand – Up Comedians

1890

Groucho Marx: 1890 - 1977.

Julius Henry 'Groucho' Marx. *One of my personal favourite comedians.* He remains a well-known figure some 40 plus years after his death. His inclusion is, mainly, for the great 'Marx Brothers' films which even today have stood the test of time: 'Monkey Business', 'Duck Soup', 'Night at the Opera', 'A Day at the Races' and many more. Groucho gained a reputation for smart ad-libs and cutting insults.

Julius Henry 'Groucho' Marx was born in 1890 in America, along with his brothers Chico, Harpo, Zeppo and Gummo (who were also in many of the films). The Marx children grew up on East 93rd Street on the Upper Eastside of Manhattan. Groucho's family was Jewish. His mother, Miene 'Minnie' Schoenberg, came from Germany. His father, Simon 'Sam' Marx, changed his name from Marrix and was called 'Frenchie' by his sons since he came from France.

Minnie's brother Al Shean (Schoenberg) was in show business, so Minnie pushed her sons onto the stage like their uncle. She pushed Chico, the oldest, to play the piano and Julius (Groucho) into singing, as he had a good soprano voice. It was from here that Groucho started to perform, and from here, the Marx Brothers were born.

Groucho became one of the most distinctive comics of his era. After his successful film career ended, he became a regular on TV and radio. His stand-up career was at the beginning of his life and the end of his career.

In 1905, in vaudeville, he started on the stage as part of 'The Leroy Trio', and later in 1909 'The Four Nightingales'. Films then took over for most of his and his brothers' lives.

A personal note, about these films, are my fond memories of being 10/11-year-old. For many weeks, on a Friday night, my dad (who was my comedy inspiration) used to wake me up between 11.30 pm and midnight to take me downstairs to watch the Marx Brothers films. As a treat, he would make me Chala (freshly baked Jewish bread) with butter and jam, along with a very strong and sweet, specially made Turkish coffee to enjoy with the film. Afterwards, my dad would send me back to bed to sleep after having jam and strong, sweet coffee.

One of my solo shows was, 'Ahhhh, I'm Jewrotic, and I blame My Jewish Mother...Who Else.' I love this story from Groucho about his mother: 'Because we were a kid act, we travelled at half-fare, despite the fact that we were all around 20. Minnie (mother) insisted we were 13.

'That kid of yours is in the dining car, smoking a cigar,' the conductor told her. 'And another one is in the washroom shaving.' Minnie shook her head sadly: 'They grow so fast.'

In 1932 his first radio programme aired, 'Flywheel, Shyster and Flywheel', and in 1947 he hosted 'You Bet Your Life' for ABC; this was on television and radio until 1950. Then from 1950 -1956, he hosted a quiz show which ran on TV and radio.

In 1972 Groucho Marx staged a live one-man show at Carnegie Hall, which was, later, released as a double album, 'An Evening with Groucho Marx' *(which I still own to this day and is very special to me, so this is why Groucho makes my list).*

Groucho always had risqué line or two up his sleeve. On one occasion, he was in a lift in Venice with a group of priests. One of them confessed to Groucho that his mother was a big fan of his. Groucho turned to him and said, 'I didn't know you guys were allowed to have mothers.'

In an interview with Playboy magazine, he was asked what he would do differently if he had his time over again. The answer, 'Try more positions.'

One day he was out working in his garden outside his house. A rich woman drove past in her Cadillac; she *stopped and summoned Groucho over, as she was in need of a gardener. 'Gardener,' she shouted over to him, 'How much does the lady of the house pay you?'* Marx replied, *'Oh, I don't get paid in dollars. The lady of the house just lets me sleep with her.'*

Famous Groucho's Quotes:

'Outside of a dog, a book is a man's best friend. Inside of a dog, it's too dark to read.'

'I never forget a face, but in your case, I'll make an exception.'

'The secret of life is honesty and fair dealing. If you can fake that, you've got it made.'

'Please accept my resignation. I don't care to belong to any club that will have me as a member.'

'Behind every successful man is a woman; behind her is his wife.'

'Anyone can get old. All you have to do is to live long enough.'

'Either he's dead, or my watch has stopped.'

'I remember the first time I had sex. I kept the receipt.'

'She got her looks from her father. He's a plastic surgeon.'

'I've had a perfectly wonderful evening, but this wasn't it.'

As I said, in between some of these amazing quotes from famous comedians, I want to add my bit of comedy stand-up as I give to you.

Groucho talked about getting old. So, I have added an old Jewish joke on the subject:

Five-year-old Emma was sitting on her grandfather's lap as he read her a bedtime story. Occasionally, Emma would take her eyes off the book and reach up and touch her grandfather's wrinkled cheek. As she stroked his cheek, she would stroke her own and then again check grandpa's. Finally, Emma spoke up, 'Grandpa, did Gd make you?'
'Yes, darling.' He replied, 'Gd made me a long time ago.'
'Oh.' She paused, 'Grandpa, did Gd make me?'
'Yes, of course, he did, my angel; Gd made you just a little while ago,' Grandpa answered.
Feeling their respective faces again, Emma turned and said, 'Gds getting better at it, isn't he?'.

Henry Churniavsky's comedy moment: VIRGINITY*

One of the most embarrassing things that ever happened to me was when I was at The Liverpool College. I was 15/16, in my GCSE and final year. We had a school disco on a Saturday night which was arranged with the all-girls school from up the road. It was an annual event for our boy's school, and it was always eagerly anticipated.

Anyway, I met a young lady, and we left the dance hall in the dark for a walk towards the Chapel. We sat down and, well, I'm not going into too much detail, but I lost my cherry! Yes, the deed was done. (This is not the embarrassing point, by the way - just hang on).

I do remember seeing someone lurking around the bushes at the time but thought nothing more. On Monday morning, I entered the gates of the school, now a man. I think there may have been a bit of strutting, to be honest, especially as my friends wanted to know more. (I say strutting - think the John Travolta – Saturday Night Fever walk but with a Jewish slant).

Anyway, it was time for registration, so no time to brag. I was sitting at my desk when the French teacher Madame Gregory entered the room. With there being only two or three female teachers in the whole school, she was adored by most of the pupils (did I mention it was all boys?). She was very petite; I mean very petite, about 4ft 6 inches in very high heels. She had long dark hair and a nice body. I must admit we got on well until I hit her!

Ok, that needs explaining. I was not bad at French, and it was nice having a female teacher. However, that summer, I got really bad hay fever, I mean really bad, with headaches and nausea. Now Madame Gregory had one really bad habit; she liked to walk up and down past the desks, and for no reason, would clip a boy over the head whenever she wanted. She needed no reason, only that she could!

On this particular day, I was suffering with my hay fever and struggling to concentrate. I noticed that Madame Gregory (I forget her first name...not even sure I actually knew her first name) was walking down my aisle with her arm out, ready to hit. As she got to me, I could see in the corner of my eye that it was my turn to get hit. I instinctively raised my large French book and tried to cover my head. At the same time, the diminutive Madame Gregory leant in, and I caught her with my book. 'Get out of my rooooom, Churney; you do not strike a teacher, you little merde! Go to your Housemaster at once.'

I tried to explain the accident and the hay fever but to no avail. 'Just get out of my sight, you stupid little boy.' Now, the issue of going to the Housemaster during a lesson invariably meant you would get the cane, usually with no questions asked.

I told my Housemaster, and all he did was laugh. 'You can't get away with anything with these French people.' But he did let me off with a caution. (This is still not the embarrassing bit).

Ok, back to registration. Madame Gregory was now doing the register and calling out the boy's names.
'Abbott?'
'Oui, Madame,' was the reply from every pupil, and you had to stand up (as if your word was not good enough).
She went on 'Abisgold.'
'Oui, Madame.'
'Barton.'
'Oui, Madame.'
'Barnard.'.
'Oui, Madame.'
'Chinn.'
'Oui, Madame.'
'Churney.'
'Oui, Madame.'
'Ahh Monsieur Churney, I 'ere you av been practising your biology dis weekend.' (THIS WAS THE MOST EMBARRASSING MOMENT) Yes, I lost my virginity and dignity.

1892

Eddie Cantor 1892- 1964

Isidore Iskowitz (Itzkowitz) – (no wonder he changed his name!) was born in New York City in 1892. He was a musical performer/comedian. His main claim to fame were his hit songs such as 'Makin' Whoopie' and 'If you knew Susie'. He also used to tell amusing stories about his wife Ida and his five daughters. His nickname was 'Banjo Eyes' due to his eye-rolling song and dance routines. He was also known as 'The Apostle of Pep,' this was due to his reserves of energy and showmanship.

His father, Mechel (Michael) Iskowitz, was a violinist, and his mother, Meta (Kantrowitz) Iskowitz, were both from Belarus. His mother died when Eddie was one, and it is not known what happened to his father, but his grandmother Esther Kantrowitz took custody of him. She died in 1917.

In 1913 Cantor married and changed his name from 'Izzy', as he was known, to Eddie to help him in his career.

In 1907, on 'Gus Edwards', he made his first public performance in vaudeville, a common breeding ground for many singers/comics of that time. In 1912 he created the character 'Jefferson' for the show 'Kid Kabaret'. He also toured with Al Lee as 'Cantor and Lee', which ended up on Broadway in a Ziegfeld post-show 'Midnight Frolic'.

In 1917 he performed at the 'Ziegfeld Follies', which he did for the next ten years in several positions: performer, composer, lyricist, sketch writer and actor.

By the 1930s, Cantor was one of the biggest radio stars in the Chase & Sanborn Hour.

In the 1950s, Eddie had his own television show entertaining a live audience and was best known for the 'Colgate Comedy Hour'.

Eddie starred in films and published books, including 'World's Book of Best Jokes.'

Eddie's Famous Quotes:

'It takes 20 years to make an overnight success.'

'A wedding is a funeral where you smell your own flowers.'

'He hasn't an enemy in the world – but all his friends hate him.'

'Marriage is an attempt to solve problems together, which you didn't even have when you were on your own.'

Henry Churniavsky's insight into marriage

My wife and I had a big row recently, and she said, 'You will be sorry. I'm going to leave you!' I replied, 'Well, make your mind up; it can't be both.'

Ok, we made up and went on a second honeymoon to New York. It was a wonderful trip. We walked and walked for hours each day. One day we went back to the hotel to have a lie-down and a rest. The walls in this hotel were not very thick; I could hear the conversation next door, and I told my wife that I had overheard what I assumed was a young girl talking to her partner. 'Oh, you're so strong,' the girl said.

I turned to my wife and said, 'You never say that to me!'

She replied, 'Well, you are not as strong as you were, are you?'

I had to agree.

'Oh, you're so romantic,' the girl said next.

So, I turned to my wife, 'You never say that to me!'

'Well, you are not as romantic as you used to be, are you?'

I had to agree, begrudgingly.

Next, I heard, 'OH my Gd, what an amazing orgasm!'

I turned to my wife and said, 'You have never said that to me!'

She turned to me and said, 'You're never there when I have one.'

Eddie talked about marriage. So, I have added an old Jewish joke on the subject:

Isn't marriage wonderful?

I married Miss Right. I just didn't know her first name was always.

The last fight was my fault. My wife asked, 'What's on the TV?' I said, 'dust!

Do you know what the Jewish punishment is for bigamy? …Two mothers in law.

Dad to his son. 'Is it true, Dad, that in some parts of Africa, a man doesn't know his wife until he marries her?'
'Son, it's not just in Africa; it's everywhere.'

Just think, if it was not for marriage, men would go through life thinking they had no faults at all.

1893

Lou Holtz 1893 – 1980

Holtz was an American vaudevillian, comic actor and theatre producer. Born in New York City in 1893, Holtz was discovered by vaudevillian Elsie Janis in San Francisco who brought him back to New York while he was still in his teens.

In 1913 he appeared in the first of many Broadway shows, 'World of Pleasure' and in 1919, 'George White's Scandals of 1919', in which he reappeared in 1920 and 1921.

In 1931 he hired Harold Arlen (who wrote the music for The Wizard of Oz in 1939) for the show 'You Said It', which ran for 192 performances.

By the 1920s, Holtz became one of the highest-paid entertainers on Broadway, reaching $6,000 per week. He was now alternating between musical comedies and vaudeville shows, where he headlined. He was also Master of Ceremonies at The Palace, and it was there that he broke all records by playing for ten weeks.

In vaudeville shows and radio, Holtz's comedy was based on telling long jokes, usually with at least one character with a strong Jewish accent. His most famous character was Sam Lapidus.

In the 30s, while still performing on Broadway, he found time to travel to London and appeared in two hits at the London Palladium: 'Laughter Over London ' and 'Transatlantic Rhythm'.

In the 1940s up to the 60s, he still performed at clubs and headlining in Las Vegas; it also got him on various TV shows including, 'The Ed Sullivan Show', 'The Tonight Show Starring Johnny Carson', 'Jack Paar's Tonight Show' and 'Steve Allen's Tonight Show'. Even at 80 years old, he appeared on 'The Merv Griffin Show'.

Holtz's final years found him at the Hillcrest Country Club in Los Angeles, lunching and sitting around a table with fellow comedians, including George Burns, Jack Benny, The Marx Brothers, Milton Berle and George Jessel...what a line-up!

Lou's Famous quotes:

As Sam Lapidus, he tells the story of him going to a grocery store for some salt. 'Do you have any salt?' he asked the owner.

'Do we have salt,' he replied. ' I got salt on dis shelf, on the other shelf, we have other salt on the shelf over there, and I can show you I have salt in the basement.'

Sam looked at him, 'Wow, that's a lot of salt; will you ever sell all this salt?'

The owner said, 'Me, no, I can't sell salt, but the man who sells me salt oy can he sell salt.'

One from the Borscht Belt

An old, Orthodox man refused his son's invitation to summer in a swanky hotel in the Catskills because he was very religious. He went to the synagogue every day and couldn't stay anywhere unless it was strictly kosher. Finally, the son arranged for him to stay in a small, Orthodox hotel where they had daily services and had kosher food. For several weeks the old man sent letters home thanking his son, saying how much he enjoyed it. Then one week - no mail. Another week no mail. The son was worried and rang to be told that his father had checked into a swanky hotel nearby. The son drove, found his hotel and room number, ran upstairs, flung the doors open only to see his Orthodox father in the arms of a beautiful young blonde woman. The son cried out in dismay, 'You, Papa! You!'

    The old man replied quickly, 'Yes, my son, but I don't eat here.'

Issy Bonn 1893 - 1977

Issy Bonn (Benjamin Levine) was born in London in 1893. At an early age Issy showed a lot of promise as an entertainer, but he was sent to Canada by his father as he disapproved. When he returned to the UK, he joined the Three Rascals in a comedy/singer act. In the early 1920s, after the 'Three Rascals', he went solo. He played music halls with a mix of Jewish Jokes and 'Schmaltzy' songs like 'Let Bygones be Bygones,' 'May I Call You Sweetheart,' and 'My Yiddishe Momme.'

Bonn started broadcasting on BBC radio programme with his 'Finkel Fetter' routine, and he toured Europe during World War II.

During the late 1940s, Issy moved back to the stage to do pantomime and took time out to write his own shows.
During the 1950s, Bonn was on Television in a version of 'Music Hall'.
He retired from the stage in the1960s and moved into theatre management.
Issy Bonn was immortalised, as his picture is on the cover of The Beatles album cover 'Sgt. Pepper's Lonely-Hearts Band'.

Issy's Famous Quote

'They told me to take the 22 bus. I couldn't find a 22, so I took two elevens.'

Issy sang about a 'Yiddishe Momme'. So, I have added an old Jewish joke on the subject:

THE TALMUD ACCORDING TO A GRANDMOTHER (BOBA/Yiddishe Momme)

The optimist sees the bagel; the pessimist sees the hole.
If it tastes good, it's probably not kosher.
20% off is a bargain: 50% off is a mitzvah.
Next year in Jerusalem. The year after that, how about a nice cruise?
Always whisper the names of diseases.
If you don't eat, it will kill me.
According to Jewish dietary law, pork and shellfish may only be eaten in Chinese restaurants.

1894

Jack Benny 1894 - 1974

Jack Benny, born (Benjamin Kubelsky) in Chicago on Valentine's day in 1894. He was often called 'Jackson' on his own show. Again, like Groucho Marx and Lou Holtz, he started as a vaudeville performer before becoming a national figure.

He was the son of Jewish immigrants Meyer Kubelsky (from Poland) and Emma (Sachs) Kubelsky (from Lithuania), who were haberdashers. He worked at the same time as the Marx Brothers and usually had to follow their 'slapstick' routine, so he fine-tuned his slow delivery act to be different.

His comic persona started with him playing the violin - badly. He was, in fact, a good violinist and a great musician, but he found out by accident that he got laughs from playing badly. Jack was one of those all-rounders, doing radio, television, film actor and violinist.

Benny's act was often portrayed as being 'mean' and 'stingy', which became his 'Shtick'.
Jack Benny was known for his comic timing; he would pause just to get laughs and even had a signature word – 'Well.'

At one stage in his career when he did his routine with a live audience, guests would come on and get introduced until, eventually, the red curtain at the back would open to reveal a room, and the routine would become a sitcom. This is universally accepted as the start of the family sitcom as it's known today. Benny's unique take in this breakthrough comedy was the start of what we know today as the sitcom era.

Jack even wrote for several comedians, including the great Bob Hope. One thing Benny quickly learned was that the longer he stared at the audience after telling a joke while saying nothing, the longer they laughed *(which, as a comedian, is a very difficult thing to do; to pause and wait)*.

Jack Benny and George Burns were close friends on and off the stage for over 50 years, and although they ripped each other apart, they remained as close as ever.

His career spanned many years in radio, TV and film; it was not until he finished his broadcasting career that Benny decided to perform as a stand-up comedian, and in 1968 recorded a comedy special at the Talk of the Town in London.

Jack's Famous quotes:

'Age is strictly a case of mind over matter. If you don't mind, it does not matter.'

'Give me golf clubs, fresh air and a beautiful partner, and you can keep the clubs and the fresh air.'

'My wife Mary and I have been married for forty-seven years, and not once have we had an argument serious enough to consider divorce: murder, yes but divorce, never.'

'A scout troop consists of twelve little kids dressed like schmucks *(idiots)* following a big schmuck dressed as a kid.'

'I don't deserve this award, but I have arthritis, and I don't deserve that either.'

Jack often talked about golf. So, I have added an old Jewish joke on the subject:

At the golf club, Manny was with some friends by the bar, and a mobile phone went off. He picked it up.
'Hello,' the voice said, 'Hello, is that you honey, are you at the club?'
'Yes.'
'Oh, I am at the shops, and I've seen that bag I really want; it's £500. Can I get it please?'
'Yes, why not!' Manny replied.
'Also, I have been to the Mercedes dealership, and that model I like is coming in. Can I please order one?'
'How much?'
'It's £50,000, please?'

'Ok, but make sure you get all the extras on it for that price.'

'I have also been rung by that estate agent, and that house we liked is back on the market for £750,000; what should I do?'

'Ok, go and make an offer of £720,000.'

'Ok, bye, honey, see you later.'

All of his friends have heard the conversation and are looking at Manny in shock. Manny turned round to the bar and said, 'Does anyone know who this phone belongs to?'

Henry Churniavsky's insight into illness

Jews love to worry. If you have a dry mouth – that's the onset of diabetes. Indigestion is the start of a heart attack. If a Jew had a bad back, his answer would be, this is the start of kidney failure.

1896

George Burns 1896 – 1996

George Burns (Nathan Birnbaum) was born in 1896. An American comedian, actor, singer and writer, he had it all. Again, like most from his era, he started in vaudeville. Burns had two careers; following the death of his beloved wife and comedy partner of over 40 years, Gracie Allen, he went back to work in show business as a single act.

He and Gracie Allen appeared on radio, television and film as a comedy duo, Burns & Allen.

His familiar trademarks, the arched brow and the cigar, were his trademarks for many years.

Burns was the ninth of twelve children to Louis (Lippe) and Hadassah (Dorah), who were both from Galicia, now Poland. Lippe was a cantor at his local synagogue as well as working as a coat presser. He died at age 47, so it meant George had to go out to work to support the family doing many different jobs.

At 14, he had already taken up smoking cigars, and he was drafted into the army in 1917 but failed the medical.

In vaudeville, Burns had to keep changing his name as he had so many acts, but none were great, and he would not get booked, but he was so determined to make it.

Burns had an amazing career starring in short films in the 1920s and 1930s, but he did not make it big until he met Gracie and created his act with her. At first, he was the funny man, but he noticed that Gracie was getting more laughs, so he switched it to make her the funny one of the double act. 'To be a straight man, you have to have a talent, develop this talent ...then you marry her, like I did.'

In 1932 Burns and Allen turned to radio, using their stage routines and sketch comedy, and turning them into a success. By 1941 Burns and his team of writers redeveloped it into a situation comedy.

The George Burns and Gracie Allen Show was on television from 1950-1958. It was a precursor for the modern sitcoms to follow.

Burns went back to films after Gracie died, and in 1975 starred in 'The Sunshine Boys', for which he won an Academy Award for Best Supporting Actor.

His stand-up career was only short, 1965-66, when he toured the US playing nightclubs and theatres with different partners (Gracie had passed away by then). He also performed a series of solo concerts, playing universities and the New York Philharmonic Hall, eventually ending up at Carnegie Hall.

George's Famous quotes:

'Show business had a lot of appeal to me. You got to wear nice clothes, you got to travel, sometimes you got paid, and it didn't really need much talent to get started in vaudeville, and if there was one thing I had, it wasn't much talent.'

'Happiness is having a large, loving, caring, close-knit family in another city.'

'It takes only one drink to get me drunk. The trouble is, I can't remember if it's the thirteenth or the fourteenth.'

'Who wants to be 95? 94-year olds.'

'Happiness? A good cigar, a good meal, a good cigar and a good woman – or a bad woman; it depends on how much happiness you can handle.'

'First, you forget names; then you forget faces. Next, you forget to pull your zipper up and finally, you forget to pull it down.'

'I can't understand why I flunked American history. When I was a kid, there was so little of it.'

'I'm very pleased to be here. Let's face it, at my age; I'm pleased to be anywhere.'

'What would I like for my 87th birthday? A paternity suit.'

'I don't eat healthy foods. At my age, I need all the preservatives I can get.'

'I was brought up to respect my elders, and now I'm 87; I don't have to respect anybody.'

'When I wake up in the morning, and nothing hurts, I know I must be dead.'

'Everything that goes up must come down. But there comes a time when not everything that's down can come up.'

'Pass me my teeth, and I'll bite you.'

'When I was a boy, the Dead Sea was only sick.'

'You know you're getting old when you stoop to tie your shoelaces and wonder what else you can do while you're down there.'

'I love old age. I never leave home without it.'

Henry Churniavsky's insight into getting older.

Getting old means you have to make choices. The other night my wife said to me, 'Let's run upstairs and make love!' My reply was, 'Well, make your mind up; I can't do both.'

I went for a pre 60th check-up. The doctor listened to my heart and said, 'Do you smoke?'
'No.'
'Do you drink to excess?'
'No'
'Do you have a sex life?'
'Yes, why?'
The doctor stopped and looked at me and said, 'Well, you have a slight heart murmur; you will have to give up half your sex life.'
'Ok, doctor, which half...the looking or the thinking?'

One of the benefits of getting older is that I now like to sleep naked. I know, not a great image to have. And I have to admit; the air hostess was not too chuffed when she looked under my blanket during a recent trip to America.

1896

Bud Flanagan 1896 – 1968

Bud Flanagan (Chaim Reuben Weintrop) was born in 1896 in Whitechapel in London's East End. His parents, Wolf Weintrop and Yetta (Kitty) Weintrop were Polish Jews. They had to flee Poland on their wedding day to avoid a pogrom.

Wolf worked as a shoe and bootmaker, sang part-time as Cantor, and also sang in pubs. Bud was one of 10 children living in Brick Lane.

By 1901 the family lived over a fried fish shop, but later Wolf went on to own a barbershop and tobacconist in Whitechapel.

Flanagan, like his American compatriots, joined a vaudeville show that toured the USA and later New Zealand and Australia. He then travelled to South Africa to perform and meet up with his brother Alec. He returned to the UK in 1915 to enlist and entertained the troops with his singing and impersonations. It's here he met a Sergeant-Major Flanagan who, besides being unpopular, was also anti-Semitic. Still, for some reason, Bud adopted his name and in 1919 formed a comedy act 'Flanagan and Roy'.

It was not until 1926 that he started a new double act, for which he is best known, 'Flanagan and Allen' (Chesney). They were booked after they established their act to perform at the Holborn Empire. This led to a successful career in records, films and Television.

In 1931 as part of the 'Crazy Gang', they appeared at the London Palladium.

Flanagan and Allen were famous for many songs, such as 'Underneath the Arches', and as a solo artist, Bud's last recording was for the sitcom Dad's Army; 'Who do you think you are kidding, Mr Hitler?'.

Bud's Famous quotes:

'No dog can go faster as the money you bet on him.'

'We dream our dreams away.'

1898

George Jessel 1898 – 1981

George Albert 'Georgie' Jessel was born in Harlem in 1898. He was an American multitalented, comedic singer, actor, songwriter and film producer. His parents were Joseph and Charlotte Jessel. By the age of 10, George Jessel was performing in vaudeville and on Broadway. His father, a playwright, died when George was young, so he had to support the family by working. His mother helped him form the 'Imperial Trio', a harmony group (she worked as a ticket seller at the theatre). At 11, he partnered with Eddie Cantor in a kid sketch, which he did until he turned 16. After a brief partnership with Lou Edwards, Jessel became a solo performer.

His most famous comedy routine was 'Hello Mama' or 'Phone call from Mama', which was a one-sided telephone conversation *(a routine which was copied by many comedians that followed, like Shelly Berman).*

In 1919 he produced his own solo show 'George Jessel's Troubles'; after that, he was then in a silent movie 'The Other Man's Wife'.

In 1921 he had a hit single, 'The Toastmaster'. He became known as the 'Toastmaster General of the

United States' and was MC for many political and entertainment shows.

By 1925 – he was a leading man on Broadway starring in 'The Jazz Singer'.
The mid-1940s saw Jessel starting to produce musicals (24 in all), and in 1946 he was a founder member of the 'Friars Club'.

The 1950s saw Jessel on the radio in the 'George Jessel Show', which later became a television series.
He was in films in the1960s, the 1970s and even in 1981 'Reds' with Warren Beatty.

George's Famous quotes:

'Marriage is a mistake every man should make.'

'This case reminds me of one in which I likened the Plaintiff's case to a colander because it was so full of holes.'

'The human body starts working the moment you are born and never stops until you stand and never speak in public.'

Henry Churniavsky's insight into children being born

I remember the day we went to have the babies. My wife was told to lay on the bed, take her clothes off, and then they pumped her full of drugs. They told her it wouldn't hurt. It made me laugh because that's exactly how I got her pregnant in the first place.

Do you remember taking your son for his first drink? I do. We went into the local, and I bought two pints of lager. He did not like it, so I drank them both. I then decided to buy two pints of ale. Again, he did not like it, so I drank them. I decided to try spirits! So, I bought two gin and tonics; still, my son did not like it, so I had to drink them both. I thought, maybe, something sweet. Two sweet martini cocktails, but again no joy. Whisky! That will be the one! Two of the best I bought, but he would not drink it! YOU know I was so pissed I could hardly push the pram home.

1901

The Ritz Brothers: Al, 1901–1965   Jimmy, 1904-1985 and Harry, 1907-1986

The Ritz Brothers were an American comedy trio performing on stage and in nightclubs and films.

The three brothers were the sons of Austrian Jewish haberdashers Max and Pauline Joachim. The fourth brother was their manager, George. They also had a sister, Gertrude; they were born in Newark, New Jersey.

Al Joachim was born 1901 (died 1965), Jimmy was born 1904 (died 1985) and Harry born 1907 (died 1986).

The brothers adopted the name 'Ritz' after Al changed his stage name. They were a dance act and added comedy to their routines; by the 1930s, they were a headline act.

In the mid-1930s, the brothers produced several films, and in some quarters were compared to the Marx Brothers.

In the 1950s, they were still appearing on stage and in nightclubs and had guest appearances on Television. They were also a top Las Vegas act. In 1958 Harry was in a sketch-comedy LP, 'Hilarity in Hollywood'.

In December 1965, Al died while appearing at the Roosevelt Hotel, New Orleans. The two remaining brothers carried on and appeared in a few more films.

Mel Brooks cast Harry in a cameo in his film 'Silent Movie'. It was his last acting role (seen leaving a tailor's shop). Mel said of Harry, 'Harry Ritz was the funniest man ever. Harry always put me away. Always.'

Sid Caesar said, 'Harry was the great innovator, his energy and sensibility opened things up for all of us. He had to be the funniest man of his time.'

Jerry Lewis added, 'Harry was the teacher.'

Ritz Brothers Famous Quote

Posing as the Three Musketeers, trying to retrieve a secret message from Milady de Winter, they turn her upside down and shake her. Numerous messages fall from her cleavage; 'She's a walking post office!' says one of the brothers.

1902

Joe E. Lewis 1902 – 1971

Joe E. Lewis was born Joseph Klewan in New York in 1902. In 1927 Lewis refused a request, and a contract, from one of Al Capone's 'lieutenants' that would have confined Lewis to only performing at The Green Mill Cocktail Lounge, which was owned by Capone. The fact was that he had been offered more money by a rival gang to appear at 'The New Rendezvous'. He was beaten so severely that it took him several years to restart his career. Capone provided Lewis with financial help, as he was fond of him, by giving him a reported $10,000, which today would be appx $150,000.

Lewis toured in the USO shows (United Service Organizations); they provided entertainment for the American Forces. He also made several films.

He was a frequent guest on the 'Ed Sullivan Show'. One of Lewis's famous friendships was with Frank Sinatra, who signed Lewis up to his record label and helped him release 'It Is Now Post Time', which was an example of his work as a stand-up comedian. Sinatra once said that even though he had recently celebrated his 50th birthday, he would have had the body of a 22-year-old man, 'If I hadn't spent all those years drinking with Joe E. Lewis.'

Joe's Famous Quotes:

'I distrust camels and anyone else who can go a week without a drink.'

'A man is never drunk if he can lay on the floor without holding on.'

'Show me a friend in need, and I'll show you a pest.'

'Show me a man with both feet on the ground, and I'll show you a man who can't get his pants on.'

'They had me on the operating table all day. They looked into my stomach, my gall bladder; they examined everything inside of me. Know what they decided? I need glasses.'

'There's only one thing money won't buy, and that is poverty.'

'Whenever someone asks me if I want water with my scotch, I say I'm thirsty, not dirty.'

'I'm still chasing girls. I don't remember what for, but I'm still chasing them.'

'I always wake up at the crack of ice.'

Henry Churniavsky's comedy moment: waking up!

I remember what my dad always said when if woken up in the morning by the phone ringing and the person said, 'Oh, did I wake you up?'

My dad would always say, 'No, I had to get up to answer the phone.

Myron Cohen 1902 - 1986

Russian born Myron came to the USA from Grodno in Russia as a little boy and grew up in Manhattan. His parents Barnett and Rebecca Feinstein Cohen also had two other sons.

Cohen started as a salesman in the garment industry in New York. He would tell jokes to his customers, who encouraged him to give up the garment business and become a professional comedian.

In the 1950s and 1960s, he was a nightclub entertainer who recorded many live albums. He also appeared on various TV programs like 'The Ed Sullivan Show'. In the 1950s, he became a top headliner. Cohen also produced a number of joke books in the 1960s, to as late as 1978. His 'shtick' was that he was able to talk in the ethnic accents of Jewish people from New York City.

Myron, with his accent, used his language to show his humour:

'aksent' – (accent)	'krank' – (ill)
'fargleybter' – (bigot)	
'briv' – (letter)	'latke' – (pancake)
'shviger' – (mother-in-law)	
'kelner' – (waiter)	'geyn' – (go)

Myron's Famous quotes/jokes:

A Jewish grandmother is watching her grandchild playing on the beach when a huge wave comes and takes him out to sea. She pleads, 'Please, Gd, save my only grandson. I beg you, bring him back.' And a big wave comes and washes the boy back onto the beach, good as new. She looks up to heaven and says, 'He had a hat!'

A member of a Chicago finance company sent a letter to Myron, which he used on stage.
'Dear Sir, after checking our records, we note that we have done more for you than your mother did - we've carried you for fifteen months!'

A waiter at Max Stage Deli was heard asking a table customer, 'Which one of you ordered the clean glass?' (The famous Max Stage Deli was by Carnegie Hall in New York.)

'Only in Las Vegas, can they have traffic lights that say – 'stop' – 'go' – and 'six to five, you'll never make it.''

A black man in a Jewish district was bewildered at the sight of Orthodox Jews.
'What the hell are they?' he asked a friend.
'Hasidim,' the friend answered. The first man retorted, 'I see dem, too, but what the hell are they?'

'When you go to Miami…you'll know it. No matter how hot it is, the women who have them will be wearing their mink coats.'

An undertaker calls a son-in-law.' About your mother-in-law, should we embalm her, cremate her, or bury her?' He says, 'Do all three. Don't take any chances.'

Henry Churniavsky's insight into my mother in law.

When my twins were born, I often heard this from my MIL, 'But that does not mean me?' The one that stands out was one Sunday late morning; the children were asleep. My wife and I were knackered. We decided to go to bed and rest. I put a massive sign on the door; 'PLEASE DO NOT DISTURB, THE WHOLE FAMILY ARE ASLEEP. PLEASE CALL LATER. WE HOPE YOU UNDERSTAND. THANK YOU'. Within 25 minutes of shutting our eyes, the doorbell rang and rang and rang. I got up to the door only to see my dear mother-in-law waiting to come in. I said, 'Did you not see the notice?' My mother-in-law (in her own words), 'What am I blind? Of course, I did, but that does not mean me, of course.' And walked into the house!

1906

Brother Theodore 1906 – 2001

Brother Theodore was born Theodore Isidore Gottlieb in 1906. A German-born American actor and comedian who was famous for his rambling monologues, which he described as 'stand-up tragedy'.

Gottlieb was born in Dusseldorf, Germany, to a wealthy family. His father was a magazine publisher. Gottlieb led a colourful early life; at 32, under Nazi rule, he was imprisoned at Dachau until he signed over the family wealth. He was deported to Switzerland for chess hustling. Eventually, a family friend Albert Einstein got him into Austria, and he also helped to get Gottlieb to England. Gottlieb was allegedly Einstein mother's lover. In 1940 after being interned in England, he left for New York.

He made several films, mainly B films, and in 1977 he provided the voice for Gollum for a TV version of The Hobbit. In the late 1940s, Theodore began his career as a monologist in California. He later moved to New York, and by the 1950s, his now dark humorous monologues had a cult following. In 1958 he had a one-person show, and during the 1960s, he was booked to perform at St. Louis Crystal Palace. He also performed at the Café Bizzare in New York's Greenwich Village.

Brother Theodore performed apocalyptic one-person shows about life, death and even broccoli. His presence of wild white hair, and with what they called a 'demon glint' in his eye, stood in Greenwich Village for nearly two decades. He was now able to get television work and made many appearances on 'The Merv Griffin Show' and 'The Tonight Show starring Johnny Carson', 'The Dick Cavett Show' and the 'Joey Bishop Show'. He retired in the mid-1970s.

The magician Dorothy Dietrich and Dick Brooks persuaded Theodore to make a comeback in Manhattan for weekend performances. He relit his success in the late 1970s by appearing on 'Late Night with David Letterman'. In the 1980s, he became a regular on 'The Billy Crystal Comedy Hour'.

He was once described as 'Boris Karloff, Salvador Dali, Nijinsky and Red Skelton…simultaneously. He died aged 94, and his headstone reads; Known as Brother Theodore/Solo Performer, Comedian, Metaphysician. 'As Long as There is Death, There is Hope.'

Brother Theodore's Famous Quotes:
'I've gazed into the abyss, and the abyss gazed into me, and neither of us liked what we saw.'

'With every failure, my reputation grows.'

'The best thing is not to be born. But who is as lucky as that? To whom does it happen? Not to one among millions and millions of people.'

'It is fatal to be right when the rest of the world is wrong.'

'My name, as you may have guessed, is Theodore. I come from a strange stock. The members of my family were mostly epileptics, vegetarians, stutters, triplets, nail biters. But we've always been happy.'

Henry 'Henny' Youngman 1906 – 1998

Henry 'Henny' Youngman was born in London in 1906, but as a child, moved to Brooklyn, New York.

Youngman was an English/American comedian who came up with the famous line 'Take my wife...please.'

Youngman started in comedy after working in a print shop where he wrote 'comedy card' one-liners. Milton Berle discovered him, and along with his wife, they became close friends. Berle once said, 'The only thing funnier than Henny's jokes is his violin playing.'

Youngman started in show business as a musician, leading a Jazz band called the 'Swanee Syncopators', and during the show, he would tell jokes. One night the comedian failed to turn up, and Youngman stood in and, as they say, 'the rest is history'.

His inoffensive, friendly style kept him going for decades. His big break was in 1937 when Ted Collins (Youngman's manager) booked him on 'The Kate Smith Radio Show'. At that time, making a living in comedy was difficult. Youngman's piece of advice was 'nem di gelt' (Yiddish) for 'take the money'.

1974 The New York Telephone Company started 'Dial-a-Joke' and over 3 million people in 1 month rang to hear a 30-second clip of Youngman's material. He never officially retired and worked until he passed away.

He did numerous gigs, small and large, and he was happy to perform anywhere. He made numerous television shows, including 'Rowan and Martin's Laugh-In'. He hosted the TV series 'The Henny and Rocky Show' with the boxer Rocky Graziano. He also appeared in films such as 'History of the World, Part I', and 'Goodfellas'.

There is a CD, 'The Primitive Side of Henny Youngman' and an autobiography 'Take My Life, Please!'

Henny's Famous quotes:

Henny's wife was the butt of many of his jokes; 'My wife said to me, 'For our anniversary I want to go somewhere I've never been before.'
I said, 'Try the kitchen!'

'My wife's cooking is fit for a king *(then gesturing as if feeding an invisible dog)* here King, here King.'

'Last night, my wife said the weather outside was fit for neither beast nor man, so we both stayed home.'

'I wouldn't say her bathing suit was skimpy, but I've seen more cotton in the top of an aspirin bottle.'

'I've got all the money I'll ever need if I die by 4 o'clock this afternoon.'

'The doctor said to me, 'You're going to live till you're 60.' I said, I am 60! he said, 'What did I tell you?''

'I've been in love with the same woman for 49 years; if my wife ever finds out, she'll kill me.'

'The secret of a happy marriage remains a secret.'

'My wife dresses to kill; she cooks the same way.'

'My wife will buy anything marked down. Last year she bought an escalator.'

'When I read about the evils of drinking. I gave up reading.'

'My grandmother is over eighty and still doesn't need glasses. Drinks right out of the bottle.'

'Just got back from a pleasure trip: I took my mother-in-law to the airport.'

'I take my wife everywhere, but she keeps finding her way back.'

Henry Churniavsky's insight into his wife being the butt of his jokes

My wife and I returned home from a party. She looks at me and says, 'Do you realise what you did tonight?'

I turned around and said, 'Ok, I'll admit I was wrong. What did I do?'

I am not very good at getting hints. Prior to a significant birthday, I asked her what she wanted for her big day. She said something that goes from 0-60 in five seconds. I guess the bathroom scales were the wrong choice.

Henny talked about drinking. So, I have added an old Jewish joke on the subject:

Two guys were sitting in a bar next to each other and started to chat.
1st guy: 'I can't help thinking from listening to you, are you from London?'
2nd guy: 'Yes, I am.'
1st guy: 'So am I, where about?
2nd guy: 'I live in Edgware.'
1st'd guy: 'Wow, so do I; what school did you go to?'
2nd guy: 'King David'
1st guy: 'OMG, so did I; what year did you leave?'
2nd guy: '1984.'
1st guy: 'I don't believe it. I also left in 1984.'
2nd guy: 'This is fate; I can't believe we have met.'

At the same time, Jack, a regular, comes in, sits down with a beer and shakes his head, 'It's going to be a long night; the Cohen twins are drunk again.'

Sally Marr 1906 – 1997

Sally Marr (Sadie Kitchenberg) was born in 1906 in Jamaica, Queens, New York. She was a stand-up comic, actress and talent spotter. To many, she is known as Lenny Bruce's mother.

She was a vaudeville and burlesque comedian, but she started as a dancer and developed a night club act based on impersonating movie stars, such as James Cagney and Humphrey Bogart. Her act was, at the time, seen as 'bawdy' and 'free lifestyle'.

She had Lenny at an early age, but as soon as Lenny started to do comedy, she decided to support him and become a talent spotter. She discovered the acts of Pat Monita, Cheech Marin, Tommy Chong and Sam Kinson.

Her role changed after Lenny's death in 1966; she raised his daughter, Kitty. She still acted and did several films, including Harry and Tonto in 1974.

Sally's Famous quotes:

'Of course, life is a bitch. If it was a slut, it would be easy.'

'Don't cry, say 'fuck' and you smile.'

Henry Churniavsky's insight into swearing (as a child).

It seems that as an older brother to two sisters, it was my responsibility to teach my younger siblings how to react to certain situations. One day, my sisters were in assembly (I did not attend this school), and a teacher was walking past the window and tapped the glass to wave at my sisters. In response, they both, at the same time (aged three and four), gave the teacher the two-finger salute. Think Churchill in reverse! Apparently, on being questioned, it was on my instruction. Never in the history of the school did a pupil who did not attend there get frogmarched in by his parents to apologise. Some people can't take a joke.

1908

Milton Berle 1908 – 2002

Born Mendel Berlinger in Harlem, Manhattan, in 1908. Milton's career spanned 80 years, working in silent films, stage, radio, movies and television. Known as 'Uncle Miltie' and 'Mr Television.' He was also known as 'The Thief of Bad Gags.' Berle made a career out of stealing other people's jokes. His mother, Sarah Berlinger, was at every stage and attended to every detail in her son's career.

When Bob Hope accused Berle of stealing his material, his mother, Sarah, said, 'My son would never stoop so low. My son stoops high.'

His stage persona had rapid-fire jokes and high energy.

Starting at age five in show business by winning a children's Charlie Chaplin contest, he appeared in silent movies, his first being, 'The Perils of Pauline.' Like many from this era, Berle, aged 12, entered vaudeville, and by the time he was 16, he was working as an MC (Master of Ceremonies).

On arriving in Hollywood at a young age, he worked with Charlie Chaplin in a Mack Sennett comedy. In 1920 he had his stage debut in an early revival of 'Floradora.'

By the early 1930s, Milton was established as a successful stand-up comedian, and a career in radio followed four years later. By the late 1940s, he gave up some well-paid nightclub spots to expand his radio career.

By 1948 Berle became the first and biggest star of a new medium - television. With shows, 'Texaco', 'Star Theatre', 'Kraft Music Hall' and 'The Milton Berle Show'. He became so famous that Tuesday nights were known as 'Berle Nights.'

By the late 1940s, Milton appeared more and more on TV, and he even won Emmy Awards.

After his TV career ended, Milton went to Las Vegas and had performed to full houses at Caesars Palace, The Sands and The Desert Inn, along with other casino hotels.

Milton entered the Guinness Book of World Records for the greatest number of charity performances made by a show-business performer.

Milton's Famous quotes:

During Milton's TV shows, he would often, for a sketch, get dressed up in outrageous costumes. On one occasion, he came out and said to a lady in the audience, 'Lady, you've got all night to make a fool of yourself; I've only had an hour.'

'If opportunity doesn't knock, build a door.'

'There's one good thing about being bald: it's neat.'

'A good wife will always forgive her husband when she is wrong.'

'A committee is a group that keeps minutes and loses hours.'

'Experience is what you have after you've forgotten her name.'

'I'm so old that when I order a three-minute egg, they ask me for the money upfront.'

'My doctor recently told me that jogging could add years to my life. I think he was right. I feel 10 years older already.'

'I took a physical for some life insurance. All they would give me was fire and theft.'

'I still have a full deck. I just shuffle slower.'

'I don't date women my own age. There aren't any.'

'The other night, I said to my wife, Ruth, 'Do you feel that the sex and excitement have gone out of our marriage?' she said, 'I'll discuss it with you during the next commercial'.'

'Your marriage is in trouble if your wife says, 'You're only interested in one thing.' And you can't remember what it is.'

'Sex at the age of 84 is a wonderful experience. Especially the one in the winter.'

'We owe a lot to Thomas Edison. If it wasn't for him, we'd be watching TV by candlelight.'

Henry Churniavsky's insight into being an MC:

Doing stand-up, I have found in a normal gig, the audience is 99% non-Jewish. They enjoy the show, but you find that 1% is Jewish, and this is the one I would pick out being an MC! You see, Jews like to complain. I remember I was an MC for a gig (now an MC is there just to keep order, to make the night run smooth, and to be a bit funny, but engage with the audience and get them ready for the comedians). I asked this man, 'Sir, are you enjoying the show?'

'No, not so much! The seat is uncomfortable; I am in a draft. Some of the comics have been funny, some not.'

I replied, 'Ok. Well, sorry for the seat, but it's not my venue; sorry, but thanks for the feedback. As a matter of interest, how do you think I am doing?'

'Well, you are trying; you could try and be a bit funnier once in a while.'

'Well, ok, I appreciate the honest feedback, Dad.'

Henry Churniavsky's insight into being the Jewish mother of famous people.

This is how I think it would be if some famous people had Jewish mothers; let's consider:

Confucius: 'What is with you, my son? All this meshuggah stuff you say, Confucius says this, Confucius says that, telling every shmuck who will listen to you. I've been telling you this for years. How about I get a bit of naches (credit) vay can't you say Confucius's mother said this?'

Alexander Bell: 'OK, OK, you invented the phone already, so vay can't you ring me more often, Mr Big Shot?'

Isaac Newton: 'Gravity, gravity, you're such a meshugganer. (Yiddish for a mad/foolish person) Just be a good boy and sit down, eat your apple and stop making such a fuss - the bump on your head is fine! Oy, I didn't make such a fuss when I gave birth to you; now that was a pain. Have I ever told you the pain you put me through?

Alexander Fleming: 'I know Alex, I know you have invented penicillin. What a Klutz (another Yiddish word for an imbecile). Look, your mother knows best, just eat your chicken soup, and dis will get rid of all your aches and pains, believe me.'

Mona Lisa: 'Mona for Gd's sake smile, all that money we spent on de braces for your teeth, and dis is the best smile you can give us? Come on, Mona, it's a portrait, not a hanging.'

Thomas Edison: 'Mazel tov Thomas. Yes, I am very proud of you; yes, I can see the light from what you call the light bulb. Now be a good boy, switch it off and go to sleep, my bubela.'

Columbus: 'I don't care vat you have discovered. You have been away for years, and did I get one letter? Not even a card.'

Moritz 'Morey' Amsterdam: 1908 – 1996

Morey Amsterdam was born in Chicago in 1908. He was an American actor and comedian. He was best known for the role of Buddy Sorrell on The Dick Van Dyke Show. He was the youngest of the three sons born to Max and Jennie Amsterdam: Jewish immigrants from Austria-Hungary.

Amsterdam started vaudeville in 1922, but as a straight man for his older brother. He was musical, and he played the cello, which he used throughout his career. By 1924 he was working in Al Capone's speakeasy. Amsterdam eventually moved to California and started writing material. His nickname was 'The Human Joke Machine'; he had the knack of being able to come up with a joke on any subject.

By the 1930s, Amsterdam was a regular on the radio; he worked on 'The Al Pearce Show', and by 1937 was MC on 'The Night Club of the Air'. He was also a songwriter penning 'Why, Oh Why, Did I Ever Leave Wyoming.'

In the 1940s, Amsterdam became a screenwriter. By 1947 he had three daily radio shows, and for a while, was on both radio and TV.

In 1948 'The Morey Amsterdam Show' ran on CBS, and in 1950 he hosted a comedy-variety show 'Broadway Open House.'

His most famous role was Buddy Sorrell on 'The Dick Van Dyke Show'. Carl Reiner, the show creator, said that he'd based the role on Mel Brooks.

Morey's Famous quotes:

'Even the police have an unlisted number.'

'A cannibal is a person who walks into a restaurant and orders a waiter.'

'According to the statistics, a man eats a prune every twenty seconds. I don't know who this fellow is, but I know where to find him.'

'People who live in glasshouses might as well answer the door.'

'My neighbour has two dogs. One of them says to the other, 'Woof!'
The other dog replies, 'Moo!'
The dog is perplexed. 'Moo? Why did you say moo?'
The other dog says, 'I'm trying to learn a foreign language.'

Henry Churniavsky's insight into owning dogs

It's not dogs I object to but to dog owners. When you are walking in the park and dog owners are talking to their dogs like they understand. 'Dixie, don't do your business in that bush?' Does the dog understand or care? To be honest, the dog is only out for four things:

1. To have a pee on the grass.
2. To have a crap.
3. Smell some dog's bums.
4. The hope of a quick shag.

So, does he really care where he craps?

I saw a dog walker with five dogs a few weeks ago, telling one of the dogs off. 'Chanel, don't play with Arthur's stick.' When did a dog understand ownership? Also, 'Dougal don't do that to Trixie?' Does this owner know if Trixie might be enjoying 'that'?

I remember when we had dogs at home, and my wife would talk to the dog like it was a real family member, 'Is daddy (ME) grumpy today?' Or ask the dog, 'Are you tired, had a hard day?' Really, he's slept most of the day, gone for a walk, pissed, crapped (and he hasn't had to pick it up!) and eaten, licked his balls: Yes, a very hard day!

1909

Mickey Katz 1909 – 1985

Mickey Katz was born Meyer Myron Katz; he was born in Cleveland in 1909; he was an American musician and comedian who specialised in Jewish humour.

Mickey was the son of Johanna and Menachem Katz and was one of five children. Menachem was a tailor. Katz, even at an early age, helped the family income by entering musical contests and, after graduating from high school, continued to support the family with money from his music. Katz was not the only Katz to go into show business; his son is the actor Joel Grey, and he was the grandfather of Jennifer Grey (Dirty Dancing fame).

During his early career, Katz was on the road, where, aged 17, he met his wife to be, Grace. She was only 14. They married three years later, in 1930.

Music was his first love; he joined several bands, eventually joining the Howard Phillips orchestra. He was unable to join the armed forces during the war, but he ran a six-man comedy and band group, 'Mickey Katz and His Krazy Kittens'.

In 1946 he was playing music in Hollywood with Spike Jones, but after a year left over an issue with money. He decided to make an English-Yiddish record, 'Haim Afen

Range', which sold so well, selling 10,000 copies in three days; that a further 25,000 were released. He eventually recorded 90 singles and ten albums for RCA and Capitol. 'Duvid Crockett, King of Delancey Street', sold 250,000 copies and got to number two in the charts. Katz led the way for other Jewish parodists, i.e. Allen Sherman.

Unfortunately, Katz's work did not appeal to all, and some people were worried that his words/music/antics would produce 'Jewish stereotypes'. Some radio stations refused to play his material, and this also deterred some venues from hiring him. Undeterred, he continued up until 1957 and then performed on and off until he died in 1985.

In 1948 he produced the English-Yiddish stage revue 'Borscht Capades' with his son Joel.

From 1951 to 1956, while he was a disc jockey, he continued to perform at nightclubs, mainly at the Bandbox nightclub. In 1952 he joined the California Friars Club and conducted their major events for 25 years. In 1953 Katz played in Las Vegas, where he had a four-year run.

His parodies included the theme from 'Moulin Rouge' – 'Where is my Heart', which became 'Where is my Pants?' 'How Much is That Doggie in the Window' became 'Pickle in the Window.'

Victor Borge 1909 - 2000

Victor Borge (Borge Rosenbaum) was born in Copenhagen, Denmark, in 1909. He was born into an Ashkenazi family; his parents Bernhard and Frederikke Rosenbaum, were both musicians. Bernhard was a violinist in the Royal Dutch Orchestra, and Frederikke was a pianist. He made my list primarily because he was a stand-up music showman, who in 1948, became a US citizen.

He was known as the 'Clown Prince of Denmark' and the 'Great Dane'; he was a genius on the piano. He started playing the piano at the age of two and did his first recital, aged eight. His first major concert was in 1926.

In 1926, after a few years as a classical concert pianist, he started his famous 'stand-up' act with piano music and jokes. He toured Europe and began telling anti-Nazi jokes. When the Germans invaded Denmark in 1940, Borge was briefly blacklisted before getting to America.

In 1940 he arrived in America, and eight years later, became a citizen. His 'comedy of music' became the running longest one-person show, with 849 performances finishing in 1956.

Even late in life, at 90, he was still performing up to 60 times a year. His trademark was repeatedly announcing his intent to play a piece of music, only to get distracted by something or someone else.

He also used to discuss the usefulness of Chopin's 'Minute Waltz' as an egg timer. He could move easily between playing Beethoven's 'Moonlight Sonata' to pop or jazz.

'Phonetic punctuation' was another trademark; he would read from a book and exaggerate all of the punctuation marks.

Victor's Famous quotes:

'Two weeks ago, we celebrated my uncles 103rd Birthday, 103 - isn't that something? Unfortunately, he wasn't present. How could he be? He died when he was 29.'

'I wish to thank my parents for making it all possible…and I wish to thank my children for making it necessary.'

'Santa Claus has the right idea. Visit people once a year.'

'Laughter is the shortest distance between two people.'

'The difference between a violin and a viola is that a viola burns longer.'

'He was happily married…but his wife wasn't.'

'My father invented a cure for which there was no disease and, unfortunately, my mother caught it and died of it.'

Henry Churniavsky's insight into Hypochondria

Hypochondria is a Jewish disease, one which has been passed on to Gentiles. Jews complain about anything and everything. Like the old Jewish joke about a waiter going over to a group of Jewish women having lunch and asking, 'Anything ok?'

My grandfather introduced hypochondria after a cruise with my Grandmother. He came off the boat and complained that there was nothing on the cruise he could complain about, and that made him nauseous, and this was when hypochondria came to pass.

1910

Jack E. Leonard 1910 – 1973

Jack E. Leonard was born Leonard Lebitsky in 1910. He was an American comedian and actor who made many television appearances.

Born in Chicago, he was the son of a Jewish tailor. In his early days, he worked as a lifeguard. His professional debut was as a dancer. In the 1930s, he joined a vaudeville troupe that played all over the country.

It was Jack Parr's 'The Tonight Show' which gave him his first break. Then he performed in Las Vegas for several years and made hundreds of television appearances on variety shows and panel shows.

Leonard's style was sarcastic and aggressive, which created what was called 'insult humour', which was picked up by Don Rickles, who once said of Leonard, 'A man who's been doing my act for about 12 years now.'

One of Leonard's trademark lines was to remove his hat, show a bald head and say, 'What did you expect, feathers?' Leonard had a strong onstage personality. He would say, 'Good evening, opponents.' As well as his trademark lines, for his act, he wore a distinctive, dark suit, usually two sizes too small, with a white hat and horned rimmed glasses.

In 1973 at only 63, he collapsed after a show at the Rainbow Room in New York, and despite surgery, never recovered.

His legacy was three albums: 'Rock and Roll for Kids Over Sixteen' (1957), 'How to Lose Weight with Fat Jack' (1964) – available on Spotify - and 'Scream on Someone You Love Today' (1967).

Jack's Famous Quotes:

On being born in Chicago, 'You know, the city where kids play robbers and robbers.'

His time as a lifeguard; 'I swam against Johnny Weissmuller *(for those of a younger age, he was the famous actor who played Tarzan in the films of the 1930s and 1940s, and also a multi gold-medal winning swimmer) a*nd he was so fast I haven't seen him since.'

'There's nothing wrong with you that reincarnation won't cure.'

1911

Belle Barth 1911 - 1971

Belle Barth, born Annabelle Salzman in 1911, was an American comedian who performed in the 1950s and 1960s. She led the way for the likes of Joan Rivers with her foul-mouthed, bawdy, irreverent humour.

Barth was the ninth child of a Manhattan merchant. She was born and raised in East Harlem, and even at an early age, was performing as a singer-pianist at the Borscht Belt hotels and nightclubs. In 1950 after her first divorce (she married five times - *must have liked wedding cake*) from Peter Barth (she kept his name throughout her career), she moved to Miami Beach. She married again in 1954 and worked the clubs in the area, occasionally travelling to New York and Chicago to perform.

In 1953, Barth was arrested because of her act. Many cases like this were thrown out; despite this, she never modified her act. She'd had, like Lenny Bruce, police in the audience, and while the clubs were, in the main small, and while she kept to one-liners, she seemed okay.

Her one trick was to use Yiddish for some of the ruder words, which many of the audience who loved her liked and the uninitiated did not understand. She even opened her own Pub in Miami, Belle Barth's Pub. Barth referred to herself as an MD, 'Maven of Dreck' or 'The Doyenne of the Dirty Ditty.'

The 1960s saw Barth perform more in New York and Las Vegas; in 1960, she signed up to the 'After Hours' record label and released a single 'If I Embarrass You, Tell Your Friends' (this single got her record of the year in Quebec). In 1961 she recorded a live set at the Roundabout Club in New York and a midnight show at Carnegie Hall. Further work followed in Las Vegas, Caesar's Palace and many more shows culminating in the early 1970s, when she ended her performances after her last at the Flamingo, where she was ill. She passed away in February 1971.

Her career saw her release nine 'adult' records, all original material and all recorded live, selling over two million records.

Belle's Famous Quotes:

Belle tells a story about a suspicious clerk at a Miami Hotel. He asks questions as he suspects the guest of being Jewish: 'Who was Our Lord?'
The gentleman replies, 'Jesus Christ.'
'Where was he born?'
The gentleman replies, 'In a stable in Bethlehem.'
'And why was he born in a stable?'
'Because a rat bastard like you wouldn't rent him a room, that's why.'

Or, the story of the man who can sing out of his arse who, when asked to do, so defecates liquid over the floor. When challenged, he says, 'Well, I had to clear my throat, didn't I?'

'Shut your honey, honey. Mine's making money.'

'The customer comes first.'

Harvey Stone 1911 – 1974

Harvey Stone was born in August 1911. An American actor, known for 'Here's Lucy' (1968), Ladies Before Gentlemen (1951) and The Tony Bennett Show (1956).

As a comedian, he was known for his army routine, the 'GI Lament'. Stone was a former shoemaker and toured army bases with Joey Adams during the war, doing military-themed comedy. He cultivated his failures as a shoe clerk to hone in on and become a stand-up and Master of Ceremonies in a seven-year stint at a cabaret called The Bowery.

After the war, he did regular stand-up on radio and became a regular at presentation houses in Chicago, Philadelphia and New York. He played at the White House for Harry Truman, and by 1949, he was on 'The Ed Sullivan Show'. It was then that he reached his top earnings; $5,000 a week doing stand-up across the country.

He was still performing into his 60s as a cruise entertainer. In fact, it was while he was on The Queen Elizabeth II in the Bahamas that he passed away. According to Jack Carter, a point of trivia is that his wife decided she did not want her Harvey left in ice on the boat; she decided that it was always Harvey's wish to be buried at sea. So they dumped him in the ocean. This was the end of Harvey Stone.

Samuel Levenson 1911 – 1980

Samuel Levenson was born in Brooklyn, New York, in 1911 into a large, Jewish immigrant family. Sam was an American humorist, writer, teacher, television host and journalist. He was known as a 'dialect comic'.

Levenson started his career as a panellist on 'This Is Show Business' (1949-1954). In 1950 he and Joe E. Lewis were the inaugural members of the New York Friars' Club. *(As a side note The Friar Club's name comes from a story that it is really based on the Yiddish word 'freier' which is colloquially used to mean a mug or a sucker, or someone who has chucked out the rules of religion to do whatever they want. It's in common usage in Israel to mean someone who's easily taken advantage of or who can't be bothered to do anything properly…thank you Rachel Creeger).*

Between 1954-1964, after appearing in many television shows, he hosted the 'Sam Levenson Show'. He has appeared on many panel shows, including 'Password', 'What's My Line' and appeared on 'Johnny Carson' throughout the 1970s.

Levenson was a Spanish teacher who also appeared many times in the Borscht Belt Hotels in the Catskill Mountains. He also wrote many books, which included 'Everything, But Money' (1966), 'Sex and the Single Child' (1969) and 'You Can Say That Again' (1975).

Sam's Famous Quotes

'If you die in an elevator, be sure to push the up button.'

'Insanity is hereditary; you get it from your children.'

'The simplest toy, one which even the youngest child can operate, is called a grandparent.'

'Lead us not into temptation. Just tell us where it is; we'll find you.'

'I admit that: my wife is outspoken, but by whom?'

'It was on my fifth birthday that Papa put his hand on my shoulder and said, 'Remember, my son, if you ever need a helping hand, you'll find one at the end of your arm.'

Sam mentions 'grandparents' Here is an old Jewish joke on grandparents.

Rebecca is 15 years old; tonight, she has a date. When she comes down all dressed up, her Bubbeh (Grandmother) sees she is wearing a see-through top, and she is wearing nothing underneath. She shouts at Rebecca and tells her she must not go out like that, looking like a tart. Rebecca, undeterred, walks out of the *door and says, 'Bubbeh, this is the 21st century; everybody lets their rosebuds show.'*

The next day, when Rebecca comes home from school, there is her Bubbeh sitting in the lounge wearing no top. Rebecca is embarrassed, and she says, 'Bubbeh, I have friends coming over, and it's not appropriate for you to...'

Her Bubbeh interrupts her and says, 'Loosen up, Rebecca, this is the 21st century. If you can display your rosebuds, then I can certainly display my hanging baskets.'

Henry Churniavsky's insight into his father

I remember my dad, who was an amazing man, but a gd awful parent, advising me aged six that because mum had taken my sisters away to Majorca with her parents, I was going to London for the weekend with him.

I was so excited. I was going to London with my dad, father and son quality time. What a treat! He turned to me, aged six, and said, 'Son, we are off to London for the weekend. I am playing bridge at night, but we will have the whole day together, so go and pack two cases for us!' I was just so excited, but really what father would get a six-year-old to pack cases! Here goes!

The next morning my dad picked up the cases. He said, 'Oh, wow, these are heavy. Ah, well!' He put them in the car. We arrived in London in record time considering there was not a full motorway between Liverpool and London in those days. Still, dad was driving an Alfa Romeo and wanted to show his six-year-old son how fast it could go, especially around corners.

See, I told you, not the best of parents; I was thrown around the back seats. Oh, yes, seat belts were not compulsory!

Anyway, we arrived late at night, and my dad carried the cases to the bedroom. He opened them, only to find that there weren't any clothes! Yep, not a shirt or piece of underwear in sight. ONLY BRIDGE BOOKS!! Yes, I had packed two full cases of bridge books, which my dad did not check. He had told me he was playing bridge at the weekend! So, we had to stay in the same clothes from Friday till Monday morning, as the shops in those days did not open at the weekend!

This trip was also memorable for other reasons too. On Friday night, upon arrival, my dad advised me that he was playing bridge in a hotel over the road, but I would be okay, aged six, in the room on my own until he returned in the early hours of Saturday morning. He said the night porter was downstairs in case of an emergency. What does that mean to a six-year-old? He also said not to wake him in the morning, but it was okay, aged six, to go downstairs when I woke up to get my own breakfast! What he did say was, 'You remember what you can't eat?'

'Yes, Dad, I won't eat the bacon.' I know it was the 1960s but, really, alone in a hotel room at six!

My dad would eventually come down to breakfast in the morning between 11.30 am – 12 noon; he would find *me in the kitchen with the staff helping to prepare the lunch—no health and safety regulations in those days.*

Phil Silvers 1911 - 1985

Ok, bear with me. Maybe Phil Silvers (born Philip Silversmith), born New York City, is not your standard 'stand-up' comedian, but this is MY book!
I have added one of my all-time heroes because, on a personal note, like the Marx Brothers, my father, who was (and still is) my hero, introduced me to so much comedy when I was young.

Each week he would give me a cassette *(yes, I'm that old)* of new comedy to listen to, and I would fall asleep every night listening to some sort of comedy. I would listen to shows like; The Goons, Monty Python, Jewish American comics, Bill Cosby (*OK, we didn't know back then!*), Jackie Mason, Shelly Berman and many more. As you know, he introduced me to many comedy programs, and one of the best was, and still is, 'The Phil Silvers Show as Sergeant Bilko'.

Silvers was the eighth and youngest child of Russian Jewish immigrants, Saul and Sarah Silver. Saul was a sheet metal worker building the early New York skyscrapers. Silver began entertaining in theatres, aged 11. At 12, he was a professional comedian. By age 13, he was working in vaudeville and as a burlesque comic. *He was known as* 'The King of Chutzpah'.

He debuted on Broadway in 1939 in 'Yokel Boy', and appeared in 'High Kickers' in 1941, and 'High Button Shoes' in 1947.

In 1951, Phil Silvers triumphed on Broadway in the show 'Top Banana', where he played the egocentric, always-busy star of a major television show (the character is said to have been based on Milton Berle). The show helped earn him a Tony award and probably helped him obtain his most famous role as Sergeant Bilko.

Between 1954 and 1959, The Phil silvers Show also won two Emmy awards.

Phil's Famous quotes:

'This is very clever; I wrote it myself.'

'You're brilliant? Say something in algebra.'

'I had an unusual beginning in show business - I started at the top.'

'Be funny on a golf course? Do I kid my best friend's mother about her heart condition?

Phil is referred to as 'King of Chutzpah' I have added an old Jewish joke on the subject:

Once there was a powerful emperor in the Far East. He was advertising for a new Chief Samurai Warrior. Only three applied for the job; a Japanese, a Chinese and a Jewish Samurai.

The Japanese Samurai stepped forward, opened a box and released a fly. He drew his sword, and with one 'swish', the fly fell to the floor, divided into two. The Emperor was delighted.

The Chinese Samurai smiled; he got up. He stepped forward, opened a box, released a fly, drew his sword and 'swish, swish' the fly fell to the floor in quarters. The Emperor was impressed.

He looked at the Jewish Samurai and said, 'How are you going to top that?'

The Jewish Samurai just shrugged, smiled and walked forward, and like the two other Samurais, he opened a box and let a fly out. He drew his sword and 'swoosh!' His sword was so mighty that a gust of wind blew through the room, and the fly let out a high-pitched sound. But the fly was still alive and buzzed around the room.

The Emperor looked at him and said, 'What kind of skill was that? The fly is not even dead.'

'Dead,' said the Jewish Samurai. 'Dead is easy. Now, circumcision...that takes skill.'

Danny Kaye 1911 - 1987

Danny Kaye (born David Daniel Kaminsky) was born in Brooklyn, New York, in 1911. A gifted mimic and physical comedian. Danny was a famous American comic entertainer, actor, singer, comedian and musician.

He was the youngest of three sons born to Jacob and Clara Kaminsky. His mother died in his early teens, and at 14, Kaye hitchhiked to Florida, from Brooklyn, with Louis Ellison as a singing duo. He returned to New York with an act known as 'Red & Blackie', which later changed to 'Toomlers at the Catskills'.

In the 1930s, Danny started as a comic entertainer in the Catskill Mountains and performed in various nightclubs around America. In 1933 he joined the Three Terpsichoreans, a vaudeville act.

By 1936, on returning stateside, Kaye worked with an American dancer, Nick Long Jr. and toured America before coming to London to play the cabaret circuit.

Danny also originated in pantomimes but soon after moved into films and music.

Kaye also had a very successful career in films, appearing in seventeen in total. He also had a successful TV and a singing career spanning over 40 years.

Kaye came to the UK in 1948 and performed at the London Palladium. He, and many others, considered this to be his finest stage performance.

Danny's Famous quotes:

'Life is a great big canvas, and you should throw all the paint on it you can.'

'I wasn't born a fool. It took work to get this way.'

'The secret of staying fresh in a show is to remember that the audience you're playing for that night has never seen it before.'

'You bet I arrived overnight. Over a few hundred nights in the Catskills, in vaudeville, in clubs on Broadway.'

Jean Carroll 1911 – 2010

Jean Carroll (Celine Zeigman) was born in Paris in 1911. She became an American actress and comedian.

She was part of a comedy dance team, Carroll & Howe (her husband). She eventually had her own sitcom between 1953-1954, 'The Jean Carroll Show', and she appeared on the 'Ed Sullivan Show' 20 times.

In 2007 – Off-Broadway, she starred in 'The JAP Show', 'Jewish American Princess of Comedy', in which she was a live stand-up.

Carroll was a trailblazer for all women who entered the male-dominated circuit of stand-up. She had impeccable timing, with an unorthodox mix of glamour and humour, and she became the first female star of mainstream comedy in stand-up—a regular headliner in many theatres and nightclubs. As a monologist, she wrote nearly all of her own material; she talked about everyday life from shopping, family and social life.

When her husband went off to fight in WWII, she said, 'If guys could tell jokes about their wives, she could about her husband.'

Jean's Famous quote:

'I'll never forget the first time I saw him, standing up on a hill, his hair blowing in the breeze, and he too proud to run and get it.'

1914

Joe E. Ross 1914 – 1982

Joe E. Ross (Born Joseph Roszawikz) was born to Jewish immigrant parents in New York in 1914. He was an American actor famed for his catchphrase, 'Ooh! Ooh!' He starred in many sitcoms *(and was one of my favourite characters in)*, including 'The Phil Silvers Show' and 'Car 54, Where are you?'.

He left school at 16 to become a singing waiter and later became an announcer, where he would add jokes; this was the start of a comedy career for Joe E. Ross.

In 1938 after appearing in the Queen's Terrace, New York, he was able to secure a 16-week contract after Jackie Gleason completed his 16-week contract. Ross then turned burlesque comic in Chicago.

After the War, Ross became an announcer-comic at Billy Gray's in Hollywood. He also worked at Ciro's nightclub in Miami Beach. Nat Hiken and Phil Silvers spotted him and cast him as Mess Sergeant Rupert Ritzik in 'You'll Never Get Rich', which became 'The Phil Silvers Show'.

1959 saw the end of 'The Phil Silvers Show', and Hiken created 'Car 54, Where are you?' and cast Ross in one of the parts. In 1966 he was in another sitcom, 'It's About Time'.

Ross also performed in many films during his career. From 'The Sound of Fury' (1950) to 'The Woman Inside' (1981).

Ross was also a prominent cartoon voice, voicing a number of characters in; 'Hong Kong Phooey' (Sgt. Flint), and 'Help...It's the Hair Bear Bunch' (as Botch) and Fangleface. He also released an album, 'Should Lesbians Be Allowed to Play Pro-football?'

Ross married eight times, all allegedly hookers!

While performing in the clubhouse of his apartment in Los Angeles in 1982, he suffered a heart attack and died.

It is thought that Andy Kaufman's alter ego Tony Clifton is based on Ross.

Joe's trademark catchphrases:

'Oooh, Oooh, Jumpin Jehosephat'.

'Do you mind?...DO-YOU-MIND?'

1916

Jan Murray 1916- 2006

Jan Murray (Murray Janofsky) was born in The Bronx, New York, in 1916. He was an American stand-up comedian, actor and game show host who started, like many Jewish comedians, in the Borscht Belt.

Born to Jewish parents, his interest in comedy began in childhood, and he would do routines, especially for his bedridden mother.

He started, aged 18, on the vaudeville stage during the 1930s; he performed in the Catskills to Jewish holidaymakers. During the 1940s and early 1950s, he became a Las Vegas performer and headlined at the famous Flamingo Hotel when it first opened its doors.

The late 1940s saw Murray move into television, appearing alongside Milton Berle, Jerry Lewis, Dean Martin and Jackie Gleason, amongst others.

The 1950s and 1960s saw Murray on television shows such as 'The Ed Sullivan Show', 'The Tonight Show', 'The Joey Bishop Show'. He also co-hosted the annual West Coast Chabad Lubavitch telethon for 18 years.

In the 1960s, Murray hosted game shows such as 'Blind Date', 'Dollar a Second' and his creations 'Treasure

Hunt' and 'Charge Account' (which was also known as The Jan Murray Show 1960-62).

During his career from the 1960s to the 1980s, Murray starred in many TV comedy and drama series, including 'Dr Kildare', 'The Lucy Show', 'The Man From UNCLE' and 'Fantasy Island', to name a few. He was also in many films, including Mel Brooks' 'History of the World, Part 1' (1981).

Murray was a keen golfer, and many of his performing partners were golfers, such as Jerry Lewis and Joey Bishop. He created comedy routines and performed them at various golf charity events.

Jan's Famous Quotes:

'Dieting: A system of starving yourself to death so you can live a little longer.'

'Dance is about movement and can be an art, but it's also about communication…with yourself, as much as with other people.'

1918

Joey Bishop 1918 – 2007

Joey Bishop (Joseph Abraham Gottlieb) was born in The Bronx, New York, in 1918. He was an American entertainer who started on television in 1948 and eventually got his own weekly comedy series. He was also famously part of the 'Rat Pack' with Frank Sinatra, Dean Martin, Sammy Davis Jr and Peter Lawford.

He was born in the Bronx but raised in South Philadelphia. He went into the US Army during WWII.

Joey was the youngest of five children to Anna and Jacob Gottlieb, who were Polish Jews. Jacob was a bicycle repairman.

While in Philadelphia, he learnt how to tap dance, do imitations, play the mandolin and the banjo. He dropped out of school at 18 and went to perform in vaudeville (with his brother). He was also part of a comedy group called 'The Bishop Trio'.

He appeared on television in 1948 as a master ad-libber, but it took time to make his name. His career took off as a duo with his brother, Maury. He appeared on 'The Ed Sullivan Show' in 1950 as part of a comedy act, and in 1957 he appeared on 'The Dinah Shore Chevy Show' and went on to perform in many more variety shows. In the

1960s, he guest-hosted 'The Tonight Show', starring Johnny Carson over 170 times. He later had his own late-night show. His persona was of a glum stand-up comic.

1961 Bishop starred in a sitcom, The Joey Bishop Show, which ran for four seasons. 1967 saw his late-night show with the same title.

The 'Rat Pack' all performed at the Sands Hotel with Bishop doing a mix of singing, dancing and telling jokes; he wrote most of the material that they all used.

Joey's Famous quotes:

'My doctor is wonderful. Once, in 1955, when I couldn't afford an operation, he touched up the X-rays.'

'Today, you can go to a gas station and find the cash register open and the toilets locked. They must think toilet paper is worth more than money.'

'The other day, I started to take a course in psycho-ceramics. What are psycho-ceramics? It's the study of crackpots.'

'Nothing is as far away as one minute ago.'

'The kick of comedy is to think quickly. It's a great kick.'

'A woman driver went through a red light. The cop stopped her and said, 'Lady, didn't you see that red light?' The woman said, 'You've seen one, you've seen them all.'

Joey talked about doctors. So, I have added an old Jewish joke on the subject:

A man was sent by his GP to see a local consultant. When he got home, he saw his wife, and she looked at him and said, 'Darling, what is the matter? You look like you have the weight of the world on your shoulders. What did the doctor say?'

'Well, he examined me thoroughly.' He replied, 'He then told me I had to take a tablet once a day for the rest of my life.'

'Oh, darling.' Replied his wife, 'What is wrong with that? It's only a tablet?'

He looked at his wife and said, 'He only gave me seven.'

Henry Churniavsky's insight into driving

You can't get anything over my wife. A few months ago, we had been to a party. I was driving home late and behind me was a police car; it flashed its lights, so I pulled over.

I turned to my wife and said, 'Don't say anything, I will sort this, ok?'

The policeman came to my window, and I opened it to speak to him.

Me: 'Good evening, Officer, everything ok?'

Policeman: 'Good evening sir, did you know a little while down the road you were speeding?'

Me: 'Sorry, I don't know the roads well here, and I do apologise; I was trying to be careful.'

Wife: 'Officer, I told him he was speeding, but he never listens.'

I turned to my wife and glared.

Policeman: 'Sir, I also noticed your brake light on the right is broken!'

Me: 'Oh really, it must have just happened today Officer, I'm sorry.'

Wife: 'I told him weeks ago about that officer; he never listens.'

I again turn to my wife, and now I point at her and hold my finger against my lips.

Policeman: 'Also, sir, I notice you are not wearing your seat belt?'

Me; 'No, I just took it off as I saw you getting out of the car as I thought I might need to get out!'

Wife: 'Officer, he never wears his seat belt; I've told him hundreds of times; he never listens.'

I turn to my wife, and I shout, 'For fuck's sake will you shut up!'

Policeman: 'Excuse me, sir.' Then he spoke to my wife, 'Does your husband often talk to you in that way?'

Wife: 'Only when he's drunk.'

1919

Red Buttons (Aaron Chwatt) 1919 - 2006

Red Buttons (born Aaron Chwatt) was born in Manhattan in 1919. A son of Jewish parents Sophie and Michael Chwatt. Michael was a milliner in Manhattan. Aaron got his name Red Buttons from the colour of his hair, and 'Buttons' was a term given to hotel porters.

In 1935 aged 16, Red got his first opportunity as a bellhop at Ryan's Tavern in the Bronx. Later that year, he teamed up with Robert Aida in the Borscht Belt. Red joined the US Army (Air Force) and was soon entertaining the troops along with Mickey Rooney. After the war, he continued entertaining on Broadway. In 1952 he was offered a television series and later films.

He became a national comedian with his 'Never Got a Dinner' routine and was on 'The Dean Martin Celebrity Roasts'. He also made numerous appearances at the Friars Club and 'Chabad' telethons. He was also often brought on and off the stage to 'Hava Nagila' (a famous Jewish song). He was proud of his Jewish roots and even said, 'I'm a Jew who is doing comedy, not a Jewish comic.'

Red's Famous quotes:

'Never got a dinner' – was used nearly every time he cracked a joke!

Uncle Remus, who said to Uncle Ben, 'You're a credit to your rice.'

Sophia Loren, whose new baby, asked her, 'Is all that for me?'

'Sure, I've gotten old. I've had two bypass surgeries, a hip replacement, new knees. I've fought prostate cancer and diabetes; I'm half blind, can't hear anything quieter than a jet engine, and take 40 different medications that make me dizzy, winded and subject to blackouts. I have bouts with dementia, poor circulation, hardly feel my hands or feet anymore, can't remember if I'm 85 or 92 but ...thank Gd, I still have my driver's licence.'

Donald Trump's mother, who said, 'Donnie! Stop playing Monopoly and get in that barber's chair!'

The captain of the Titanic, who said to room service, 'Who sent for all this ice?'

Eve, who asked Adam, 'Does this fig leaf make me look fat.'
Adam, who said to Eve, 'What do you mean you have nothing to wear?'
Eve, who said to Adam, 'What do you mean the kids don't look like you?'

Moses, who said to the children of Israel, 'Wear your galoshes (waterproof overshoe): I never did this trick before.'

Henry Churniavsky's insight into the bible

To get more people interested in the bible, maybe we need to make it more of a TV Show.

Adam & Eve: *If Adam and Eve were a 21st-century story and Adam had eaten the apple and blamed the snake, they would now appear on the 'Judge Rinder Show'.*

Noah: *A new TV show: Neighbours from Hell.*
Here is Noah, the day after chatting to Gd, he is now, daily, checking the weather reports hourly. His neighbour comes over and asks, 'Hey Noah, what's with all the wood you've had delivered? I mean, it's a lot and a bit of an eyesore. Are you having a big barbeque?'

'Sorry mate,' says Noah. 'I will try and get it moved asap, ok?'

'Ok, but make sure you do as I can't get into my driveway.'

A few days go by, and Noah is now collecting some of the animals. His neighbour comes around again, 'Hey, Noah, what the F! man.' Now your rehoming animals, what's going on?'

'Sorry, can't tell you it's a secret.'

'Oh man, you have to give me a hint, my wife is doing her nut?'

'Ok, do you own rubber rings?'

The neighbour looks at him, 'You have gone mad, mate. So, what are you going to do about the animals? Who is going to clean up all that shit from the elephants in our path? It's a disgrace. And the squawking from those two parrots, can't you shut them up? They have kept us awake all night. A mosquito has bitten my wife. Don't you need some sort of licence to keep all these animals?'

Noah just smiles and says, 'Don't worry, neighbour, we will be gone soon.'

Moses: Technically, Moses was the first man to download files from the cloud using a tablet.

Was Moses a supreme athlete? At the age of 80 (the bible says he lived to 120!), he climbed a mountain to talk to Gd. To be honest, that was a bit of a 'shmuck' (idiot) thing to do, really, as Gd is everywhere, and if Gd did ask him, it was a bit unfair considering his age!

Was Moses a perfectionist? Why did Moses not just write them down on some parchment? No, too easy. He chisels them in marble. Marble was available at the top of the mountains back then! He then has to 'shlep' (carry) two heavy stones back down from the top of the mountain, and then when he gets back has to kick ass over a golden calf! A new show called 'I Did it My Way'.

Judah & Tamar Not the most popular stories of the bible, but one of the stories would definitely make a good soap series.

A story of two families, well, a family and a femme fatale!

On one side, we have Judah and his family of three sons, Er, Onan and Shelah. On the other side, the female temptress, Tamar.

Tamar marries the eldest of Judah's sons, Er, who unfortunately dies. Judah wants the family line to continue. Onan is obliged to marry his brother's widow, so Judah asks him to get Tamar pregnant. I'm not sure if Onan had a choice, but it is the first time we read in the bible about 'coitus interruptus'. Apparently, this angered Gd (I know now not to do this!), and Onan died.

Judah, the father now of only one son, stops the wedding of his third son Shelah to Tamar. (I bet he was glad of this!). Much to the annoyance of Tamar, who responds by dressing up as a prostitute (yes, this is in the bible) and seduces her father-in-law (who does not do 'coitus interruptus'). Judah ends up getting Tamar pregnant with twins! Well, you got to hand it to her; she definitely likes this family tree! If the Jeremy Kyle show was still on, this would have been a cracker of a show.

1921

Rodney Dangerfield 1921 - 2004

Rodney Dangerfield (Jacob Rodney Cohen) was born in Babylon, Long Island, New York, in 1921. He was an American stand-up comedian, actor, producer, screenwriter, musician and author. He was the son of Dorothy 'Dotty' Teitelbaum (she was born in the Austro-Hungarian Empire) and the vaudeville performer Philip Cohen, whose stage name was Phil Roy. Rodney's dad was never around, and he would only see him a few times a year. Because of this, Dotty, Rodney and his sister moved to Queens.

He was best known for his stand-up for his self-deprecating one-liner humour and his catchphrase 'I get no respect.' Despite this catchphrase, he was one of the most respected entertainers of the day. He used monologues on his self-deprecating themes.

At 15, he wrote for other stand-up comedians while also performing in Ellenville, New York. At 17, he was performing as an amateur in nightclubs.

By the age of 19, he changed his name to Jack Roy but struggled financially, eventually taking up a day job in the mid-1950s to support his family. One of his famous lines, when he gave up show business, was, 'At the time I quit, I was the only one who knew I quit.'

By the 1960s, he was missing the limelight. While still working in his day job, he, like many others, cut his teeth in the Borscht Belt and the resorts of the Catskill Mountains.

He decided to get a new image to set him apart from other comics, and this was when Rodney Dangerfield was born. His break came in 1967 on the 'Ed Sullivan Show' where he was a last-minute replacement and became the hit of the show. He became a regular on 'The Dean Martin Show' and the 'Tonight Show' in 1972/1973.

His act took him to late-night talk shows in the1960s and1970s, and he eventually became a headline act in Las Vegas. He performed on the 'Ed Sullivan Show' 16 times and did an unprecedented 70 spots on the 'Johnny Carson Tonight Show'.

In 1969, he and his friend Anthony Bevacqua teamed up to open Dangerfield's Comedy Club in New York. He did it so he would not need to travel too far (I did the same in Liverpool by opening my own little comedy club, CUE comedy, for the same reason). Unlike mine, Rodney's club was a huge success and has been for over 50 years. He also helped many other comics, including Jerry Seinfeld, Tim Allen, Roseanne Barr, Bill Hicks and many more. He also helped Jim Carrey with his rise to stardom by getting him to open at his club. He also toured with Jim for a couple of years.

A career in films followed, and a comedy album (1981) which won a Grammy Award - 'No Respect.'

Dangerfield was also nominated for a Grammy in 1985 and 1987– 'Rappin Rodney' & 'Twist & Shout'.

1991 – AGVA awarded Dangerfield – Male Comedy Star of the Year. 1995 – American Comedy Award – Creative Achievement Award. 2003 – Received a Lifetime Achievement Awards at The Commie Awards

Dangerfield was listed as No.36 out of the '50 Funniest People' by 'Entertainment Weekly'.

Dangerfield was also in the television programme 'The Simpsons' as Mr Burns' son.

A trivial fact for you; he appeared as himself in Billy Joel's video – 'Tell Her About It'.

Rodney's Famous quotes:

'When I was a kid, my parents moved a lot, but I always found them.'

'I walked into a bar the other day and ordered a drink. The Bartender says, 'I can't serve you.' I said, 'Why not? I'm over 21!' He said, 'You're just too ugly.' I said, as always, 'Boy, I tell you; I get no respect around here''.

'My Fan club broke up. The guy died.'

'Last week, my house was on fire. My wife told the kids, 'Be quiet; you'll wake up, Daddy.''

'I was ugly, very ugly. When I was born, the doctor smacked my mother.'

'You know you're getting older if you have more fingers than real teeth.'

'I'm at the age when food has taken over the place of sex in my life. In fact, I've just had a mirror put over my kitchen table.'

'I told my psychiatrist that everyone hates me. He said I was being ridiculous; everyone hasn't met me yet.'

'My wife and I were happy for 20 years…then we met.'

'I told my wife I want to be cremated. She's planning a barbecue.'

'My wife is a bad cook; she is the worst cook in the world. She gave my son alphabet soup, and he spelt out, 'help'. She is so bad; how can toast have bones?'

'If it weren't for speed bumps, pickpockets and frisking at airports, I'd have no sex life at all.'

'I'm on a new diet of Viagra and prune juice. I don't know if I am coming or going.'

On entering a hospital for heart surgery, he again came up with a classic line when asked how long his stay would be, 'If all goes well, about a week. If not, about an hour and a half.'

'At my age, I like threesomes - in case one of us dies.'

Rodney talked a lot about sex. So, I have added a few old Jewish jokes on the subject:

What is a Jewish ménage-a-trois? Two headaches and an erection.

What is a Jewish nymphomaniac? A wife who does her hair and sleeps with her husband on the same day.

What do you call the nipple on a Jewish wife's breast? The tip of the iceberg.

Henry Churniavsky's insight into sex

I remember talking to the girlfriend about experimental sex. Well, I told her she would need to change her 'safe word', as I felt her safe word 'harder' was not really helping matters! She was also into rough sex - I mean, what is this 'rough sex'? I'm an old Jewish *man, the only rough sex I remember was getting carpet burns as a teenager.*

She went on during sex by saying, 'Hurt me, hurt me'. WTF does that mean? Well, me apparently, telling her that her sister was better at sex was not what she meant!!

1922

Jack Carter 1922 – 2015

Jack Carter (Born Jack Chakrin) was born in New York in 1922. He was an American comedian, actor and television presenter. He had a long-running comedy act akin to Milton Berle and Morey Amsterdam.

He was born to a Russian-Jewish family who owned a candy store. Carter served in the United States Air Corps during World War II. He started television work as a host on 'Cavalcade of Stars', he was then lured to NBC to host his own show 'The Jack Carter Show'.

His days on the road started with 'The Major Bowes Amateur Hour' group, where he would do impressions. He was later known as 'The King of Vancouver' (a city he loved), where he met Morey Amsterdam.

His only major Broadway appearance was opposite Sammy Davis Jr. in the 1956 musical 'Mr Wonderful'. He replaced Phil Silvers in 'Top Banana', and he was a frequent guest on 'The Ed Sullivan Show', where he would also do impressions of the host. Carter appeared alongside his wife in 'The Joey Bishop Show'. He was also in a number of television shows and did voice work for 'King of the Hill' and 'Family Guy'.

In the 1970s, he appeared in the 'Dean Martin Celebrity Roasts' many times.

Jack's Famous quotes: (He used a lot of *Yiddish* in his act on stage)

'People spend their lives searching for their one true love, their other half. I found mine in college, dancing in a fraternity house driveway. Lucky for me, she found me right back.'

'What's the matter with kids today?'

'A man sees a (*'zaftig'*) fat lady carrying a duck. The guy says, 'What are you doing with that pig?' The fat lady snorts, 'That's not a pig; it's a duck.'
The guy says, 'I'm not talking to you. I'm talking to the duck.''

'If you like to spend your *(vakatsye)* vacation in out-of-the-way places where few people go, let your wife read the map.'

On Milton Berle. 'Milton adored me. I'll never forget the *(ershter)* the first time I met him. I walked into a New York restaurant, Lindy's, and Milton ran up to me; he took me aside - and left me there.'

'When you did Ed Sullivan, you couldn't say *(pupik)* bellybutton.'

'Canada ran out of silicone, and the girls up there are using hamburger helper.'

To a heckler, 'I couldn't warm up to you if we were cremated together.'

'I'm not a has-been!' He would say to an audience; he would pause and then 'I'm a never-was!'

Carter, it is said, was a (*zorgn zikh*) a worrier. 'A comedian doing a solo routine is selling himself, and if the *(oylem)* audience does not laugh, the performer feels a sense of personal rejection. That hurts, and that's why clowns must be the saddest people on earth.'

In the Catskills, he talked about Jewish mothers and dealing with old age. 'I told her to act her age, so she died.'

Henry Churniavsky's further insights into his mother

The last major issue was her parental guidance. My mum knew how to get me and my sisters to be good and behave. Besides the stare, which, like Lot's wife in the bible, could turn you into a pillar of salt, there was also the language she used for parental guidance.

If we did anything wrong, 'YOU want to kill me, your ONLY mother. Or, 'YOU do this because you only want me to suffer...DON'T you.' She has also used the line 'Why don't you just stab me, and it will be all over? You know I hate to suffer.' Also, 'Come here, yes, you, come here. I need you to take the knife from my back and then PLUNGE into my heart; you know you want to!" The best, however, *'Go on, carry on if you want to kill me, your mother. The one person who spent 24 hours with no pain relief to deliver you into this world. I brought you into this world. I can take you out, you know.' I was only 3!!!*

No wonder my sisters are in therapy!

Sid Caesar 1922 - 2014

Sid Caesar was born in Yonkers, New York, in 1922. Sid was an American comic actor and writer; he was more of a 'sketch' comic as opposed to a stand-up comedian. Caesar makes this list as he was, in the 1950s, a very influential figure to many comedians of this era. He had many comics writing for him early in his career, such as Mel Brooks, Neil Simon, Carl Reiner, Woody Allen and others.

Caesar relied on body language, accents and facial movements with dialogue. He was known as 'One of the most intelligent and provocative innovators of TV'.
Caesar was the youngest of three boys to Max and Ida Ziser, Jewish immigrants from Poland. They ran a restaurant, and it was here that a young Sid Caesar learned to copy the language and accents of his parents' clients. This is where he started out with his brother David and where he got the knack for comedy.

In the late 1930s, Caesar was at the Catskills Mountains in New York, and besides playing in a dance band, he performed comedy shows three times a week.

Later he toured with 'Tars and Spars', which became Caesar's first major gig as a comedian. One performance he performed in four different languages.
Caesar made a career in TV and film, for which he became a household name; his live weekly television

show, 'Your Show of Shows', was watched by 60 million people and 'Caesar's Hour' was a one-hour sketch/variety show. Caesar appeared in many well-known films including 'Grease' and 'Grease 2', 'It's a Mad Mad Mad World', 'Silent Movie', 'History of the World, Part 1' and 'Cannonball Run 2' to name a few.

Sid's Famous quotes:

'Comedy has to be based on truth. You take the truth, and you put a little curlicue at the end.'

'The guy who invented the first wheel was an idiot. The guy who invented the other three, he was a genius.'

'The trouble with telling a good story is that it invariably reminds the other fellow of a dull one.'

'In between goals is a thing called life, that has to be lived and enjoyed.'

Sid talked a lot about life (work). So, I have added an old Jewish joke on the subject:

Two beggars are sitting on the pavement in Ireland. One is holding a large cross, and the other the Star of David. Both are holding out hats to collect any contributions. As people walk by, they snub the guy holding the Star of David but drop money into the other guy's hat. Soon, one of the hats is really full while the other is empty.

A priest sees this and walks over to the men. He turns to the man holding the Star of David and says, 'Don't you realise that this is a Christian country?' You will never make any money in this country holding a Star of David.'

The guy looks up at the priest, turns to the man holding the cross and says, 'Hymie, look who is trying to teach us marketing.'

Carl Reiner 1922 - 2020

Carl Reiner was born in The Bronx, New York, in 1922. He was an American comedian, actor, director and screenwriter. He aimed to be a Shakespearian actor. His parents Irving and Bessie Reiner, were Jewish immigrants from Austria and Romania; Irving was a watchmaker. Carl followed his uncle Harry Mathias into the entertainment world.

In 1943 Reiner was drafted into the Army Air Force. When Reiner was transferred to France, he trained as a French interpreter. While he was stationed there, he had his first experience as a director by doing 'Moliere', a play in French.

He was later posted to Hawaii, and it was there he entertained the troops. He left the army in 1946.

After the army, Reiner performed in many Broadway musicals and eventually, in 1950, was cast into Sid Caesar's show, where he worked as a writer, with Mel Brooks and many more.

Brooks and Reiner formed a comedy double act, where they played a 2000-year-old man, from which they went on to make comedy albums and a TV animated special. Reiner was the perfect straight man to Brooks's performance.

Carl Reiner developed TV shows and films. He also played a big part in helping Steve Martin by directing and co-producing many of his films.

Carl maybe not your typical stand-up comedian, but his influence, especially with Mel Brooks and others, deserves mention.

Carl's Famous quotes:

'A lot of people like snow. I find it to be an unnecessary freezing of water.'

'The absolute truth is the thing that makes people laugh.'

'Lust is easy. Love is hard. Like is most important.'

Carl talked a lot about love. So, I have added a few old Jewish jokes on the subject:

Benny and Becky were sitting in a romantic restaurant, and he turns to her and says, 'Becky, I'm going to make you the happiest woman in the world.' Becky looks at him and replies, 'I'll miss you.'

I hear the economy is so bad now that Jewish women are starting to marry for love.

A study has been done at Oxford University on why Jewish women like Chinese food so much. The study revealed that it is due to the fact that WON TON spelt backwards is NOT NOW.

1923

Dick Shawn 1923 – 1987

Dick Shawn (Richard Schulefand) was born in Buffalo, New York, in 1923. Shawn was an American actor and comedian who played a variety of supporting roles.

In his film career, he played Sylvester Marcus, son of Mrs Marcus (Ethel Merman), in 'It's a Mad, Mad, Mad, Mad World' (1963). He also played the easy-going L.S.D. in the fictional musical 'Springtime for Hitler', in **Mel Brooks's** movie – The Producers (1968), amongst other films.

He performed stand-up for over 35 years all over the world. He also had an award-winning one-person show, 'The Second Greatest Entertainer in the Whole Wide World'.

Performing in over 30 movies and seven Broadway productions, Shawn also had time to do many television appearances and even toured his one-person show. Shawn has also filled in for Johnny Carson on the 'Tonight Show'.

It is said that Shawn inspired Andy Kaufman; it has been suggested that Andy's act, which at times baffled and bemused his audience, was inspired and even lifted from Dick Shawn.

One of the unusual aspects of his stage show was that he would sometimes have bricks/debris on stage, and when the show started, he would emerge from the rubble, unknown to the audience. His act would then go on with a monologue or a rant about himself. During the interval, he would lie on the stage on his back and not move until the second part of the show started. His act would also have singing, dancing and juggling with a persona called 'Mr Fabulously Fantastic Jr'.

In 1987 during a performance in San Diego, Shawn suffered a fatal heart attack and died on stage.

Dick's Famous Quotes:

'If you gave wings to a cat, it would not condescend to be a bird; it would be an angel.'

'I think of my relationship with any audience as a love affair. It lasts only a little while, but I always look forward to a happy ending. For both of us.'

Larry Storch 1923 -

Larry Storch (Born Lawrence Samuel Storch) was born in New York in 1923. Storch is an American actor, comedian and voice actor who is best known for his comic television shows.

Storch was the son of Alfred Storch, a realtor, and mother Sally, a telephone operator. Due to hard times in the family, Larry never graduated and found paid work as a stand-up comedian.

Being a stand-up comic led Storch to a number of appearances on television shows such as; 'Car 54', Where are you?', 'Get Smart', 'Sergeant Bilko', 'Columbo', 'I Dream of Jeannie' and many other shows. His most famous role was in 'F Troop'.

Storch also appeared in many variety shows: 'Sonny and Cher', 'Laugh-In', 'Ed Sullivan', 'Johnny Carson' and the 'Steve Allen Show'. This eventually led to his own, 'The Larry Storch Show'.

As an impressionist, Storch could do 100s of voices which helped him when he did cartoons. He also appeared in over 25 Hollywood films from 'Who Was That Lady' (1960) to 'A Fine Mess' (1986).

Back in the 1950s, he first performed on Broadway in 'Who Was That Lady I Saw You With?'. Later in his career, he returned in shows like 'Breaking Legs', 'Porgy and Bess', 'Arsenic and Old Lace' and 'Annie Get Your Gun'.

In 2004, he was in 'Sly Fox' with Richard Dreyfuss, and in March 2008 celebrated 50 years performing on Broadway. In 2012 Storch appeared in 'Love Letters'.

Storch recorded a comedy album 'Larry Storch at the Bon Soir' in the 1960s.

Larry's Famous quotes

'Sometimes, I walk out on stage, and you can hear from the balcony, 'Hey, Agarn!' It still tickles me after 40 years. They don't make them like F ‑Troop (19650 anymore!).

'The most money I ever made was on a McDonald's hamburger commercial.'

'I'll never forget what Edward Everett Horton said to me, 'Promise me, Larry, you will never grow old.' I've tried my best to use that advice.'

Henry Churniavsky's insight into his getting old

They say 60 is the new 50; well, it's bullshit! Let me explain. I was driving the other day when the police stopped me, and the policeman came to my window. 'Sir, did you know you were doing 60 in a 50 zone?'

'Ah, officer, so sorry, but have you not heard that 60 is the new 50?'

The policeman looked at me and said, 'Are you some sort of comedian?'

'Well, officer, it has been said before.'

I got a speeding ticket; that bastard had no sense of humour.

1924

Buddy Hackett (1924 – 2003)

Buddy Hackett (Leonard Hacker) was born in Brooklyn, New York, in 1924. He was an American actor and comedian who started his career at the Pink Elephant, Brooklyn Club. From there, he made appearances in Los Angeles and Las Vegas.

Buddy was one of two children born to Anna and Philip Hacker. Anna worked in the garment industry while Philip was a furniture upholsterer and a part-time inventor.

He was one of the most beloved stand-up comics of his day. He was also one of the raunchiest; his popularity was that he could be lovable and dirty. His stand-up routine was based on 'The Chinese Waiter', which he performed at the Catskills, and on television in 'Laff Time' in 1944.

He also acted on Broadway in 'Lunatics and Lovers', which got him two television specials.

His movie career began in the 1950s, and he was in the films 'The Music Man', 'It's a Mad Mad Mad World', 'The Love Bug.'

His television career followed on from programs such as the Johnny Carson version of 'The Tonight Show'. His brash and often blue jokes made him a hit with the audience. From 1956 he was a regular on 'The Jackie Gleason Show'. He continued to be on television into the1970s, and later in life, he had a recurring spot on the

'Late Late Show' with a segment called 'Tuesdays with Buddy.'

Hackett was in a situation comedy (1956-1957), and he also performed on Broadway in many shows like 'I had a Ball' and 'The Music Man'.

In 1989 Buddy was a voice actor in the Disney film 'The Little Mermaid'.

Buddy's Famous quotes:

'I've had a few arguments with people, but I never carry a grudge. You know why? While you're carrying a grudge, they're out dancing.'

'I've had a good day when I don't fall out of the cart.'

'Golf is more fun than walking naked in a strange place, but not much.'

'As a child, my family's menu consisted of two choices: take it or leave it.'

Henry Churniavsky's insight into eating out/menus

Have you noticed, now, when you go out to eat, that all menus have abbreviations next to most of the food on the menu? For instance: V is now showing for Vegetarian, VV – Vegan, GF – Glutton Free and sometimes H for Hallal (Not seen many K for Kosher!). I was recently in a Liverpool restaurant, and every item on the menu was FN.

FN, not seen this before, I thought, so I called the waitress over, and I asked her what FN was for. She looked at the menu, looked at me, then back at the menu, and said in a strong scouse accent, 'Fuckin' Normal.'

Allan Sherman 1924 - 1973

Allan Sherman (Allan Copelon) was born in Chicago in 1924. His main claim was that he was a song parodist. He was a comedy writer, TV producer, singer and actor.

Allan's parents were Percy Copelon and Rose Sherman. Percy was an auto mechanic and race car driver. After Allan's parents divorced, he took his mother's maiden name because they moved around so much, he attended 21 schools!

He was the most successful musical humourist in pop history, entering show business as a writer for Jackie Gleason and Joe E Lewis.

Sherman is most famous for his songs of the 1960s, which included 'Hello Muddah, Hello Faddah'.

His TV game show 'I've Got a Secret' ran from 1952-1967. He was not classed as a stand-up comedian, but his album 'My Son, the Folk Singer' (1962) had over a million sales.

Later in his career, from 1966, Sherman performed in front of live audiences.

Allan's Famous quotes:

'When the great history of trouble is written, my family will stand extremely high in the table of contents.'

'You want to fall in love with a shoe, go ahead. A shoe can't love you back, but, on the other hand, a shoe can't hurt you too deeply either. And there are so many nice-looking shoes.'

'Anyone who calls it 'sexual intercourse' can't possibly be interested in actually doing it. You might as well announce you're ready for lunch by proclaiming, 'I'd like to do some masticating and enzyme secreting'.'

On Adultery

'Adultery, which is the only grounds for divorce in New York- is not grounds for divorce in California. As a matter of fact, adultery in Southern California is grounds for marriage'.

Henry Churniavsky's insight into adultery (well, having a girlfriend).

Not wanting to point fingers, but do you sleep with a snorer? I do, but then again, I also snore. It's a thing that has grown worse over the years. It's part of life. I snore, even when I'm awake. My wife has a great way of stopping me from snoring. She will bang the bed next to me so that I wake up; then, she will pretend to be asleep. I know she's pretending because I know how she snores when she is asleep, and it is not the same. I won't say anything, of course, just turn over. A fact for you. Did you know we all have an individual snore? Oh, yes, we do. I know this because my girlfriend's snore is so different from my wife's. However, the girlfriend's sister's is very similar to her sister's, and this has led to one or two embarrassing moments that I am not willing to talk about now.

My wife, after 30 years of marriage, said I needed to be more romantic. So, I joined Tinder and got a new girlfriend!

Jackie Vernon 1924 - 1987

Jackie Vernon (Ralph Verrone) was born in 1924. He was an American stand-up comedian, actor and voice actor, best known for the voice on 'Frosty the Snowman'.

Vernon was a gentle, low key, self-deprecating comic. He was known as 'The King of Deadpan'.

In the early 1950s, Vernon would go around the country performing wherever he could, even strip joints. Eventually, he gave New York a go, and it was there he was picked up by Willie Weber's manager. In 1963 Steve Allen invited Vernon onto his show 'Celebrity Talent Scouts'. It was from here his career took off.

The 1960s saw Vernon open for Dean Martin and Judy Garland, and he found a regular spot on 'The Merv Griffin Show'.

Vernon was also musical; he could play the trumpet and the cornet and often used these as props in his act. It was when he blew the cornet he would say, 'I think I hurt myself!'

During the 1970s, he appeared on Celebrity Roasts; on many of these, he would use X-rated style jokes about people engaging in sexual depravity, and he would often end with, 'And I thought to myself...what a neat guy.'

One famous story about Vernon was his fascination for Charlie Chaplin; he used to write letters to Chaplin but never got a reply. One night while appearing in Las Vegas, he was told that Chaplin would be in the audience. Vernon wanted to meet him and found out where Chaplin was eating prior to his gig. Vernon went up to Chaplin and introduced himself; Chaplin allegedly interrupted him and said, 'Of course, Jackie Vernon. Tell me: why did you stop writing?'

Vernon's routines were usually personal; his rocking horse died (again), or his wife could not find her recipe for cold cereal that morning. He sometimes walked around the stage showing imaginary slides by saying to the audience, 'click-click'.

Jackie's Famous quotes

The opening line, 'To look at me now, it's hard to believe I was once a dull guy.'

'We lived in a small town built on a one-way street. If you miss it, you have to drive all the way around the world to get back.'

'I was so unpopular as a kid, Dale Carnegie (an American writer) once hit me in the mouth.'

'I called Dial-a-Prayer, and they hung up on me.'

'When I was a kid, I went around on the beach, kicking sand in my own face.'

'At parties, I was such a wallflower; I sat in the closet, memorising the labels on coats.'

Gary Morton 1924 – 1999

Morton (Morton Goldaper) was born in New York City in 1924. He was an American stand-up comedian; he mainly performed in the Borscht Belt in New York. Due to him not expanding his arena, he is not as well-known as his peers and was an opening act for many major artists at the time, including Tony Bennett.

Morton was more famous for marrying Lucille Ball and was the warm-up act for the 'Lucille Ball Show'. He was happy to be referred to as 'Mr Lucille Ball.'

1925

Lenny Bruce 1925 – 1966

Lenny Bruce (Leonard Alfred Schneider) was born in Mineola, New York, in 1925. He was an American stand-up comic, social critic and satirist.

Lenny's parents divorced when he was ten, and he lived with various family members over the next ten years. His father was British born Myron 'Micky' Schneider, a shoe clerk. His mother is already mentioned in a previous chapter, Sally Marr, a stage performer and an enormous influence on Bruce's life.

Lenny Bruce had his own genre (of comedy). He was reckless, visionary, he defied conventions, the law and the system, but in the end, he was taken down by it. Despite dying young (an overdose just before his 41st birthday), Bruce changed the face of stand-up for many generations of comedians who followed. He was a unique talent. His stand-up routine, which was free-style, covered politics, religion, sex and vulgarity. He revolutionised his profession, turning comedy into a serious, political tool.

In the 1950s, Bruce stormed The Citadel and tore the walls off convention with 'The Original Rebel'.
In 1964, Bruce was convicted in an obscenity trial (and was later pardoned).

In 2017, The Rolling Stone magazine ranked Bruce as 3rd behind Richard Prior and George Carlin as the best stand-up of all time.

In his early career, Bruce managed to get an 'undesirable discharge' from the Navy as his officers objected to one of his comic performances, in drag, to which Bruce said he was experiencing homosexual urges. The discharge was later changed to 'unsuitability to the Naval service'.

In 1957 Bruce was booked into the 'Slate Brothers Nightclub'; he was fired on the first night due to his 'blue' material. This led Bruce to do his first solo album 'The Sick Humour of Lenny Bruce'. By now, Bruce was branded a 'sick-comic' and was, essentially, blacklisted from TV and only performed occasionally.

In 1961, at Carnegie Hall, he produced one of his memorable performances, which led to a 3-disc set. His routines included 'The Palladium', 'Hitler and the MCA', 'Religion Inc'. He exposed racism and bigotry – 'White Collar Drinks', 'How to Relax Your Coloured Friend at Parties', and he satirised movies – 'The Defiant Ones'.

Late in 1961, he was arrested for obscenity at the Jazz Workshop in San Francisco, and again in 1962 at the Gate of Horn Folk Club in Chicago.

In 1962 Bruce visited Australia and gigged, but this was short-lived and surrounded by controversy.

In 1964 Bruce appeared twice at Café au Go Go in Greenwich Village, New York. There were undercover police in the audience, and he and the club owners ended up arrested for the obscene performance, for which he was found guilty. He was sentenced to serve four months in a workshop. Bruce, unfortunately, died before the appeal was decided.

His lone benefactor at this time was the rock and roll producer, Phil Spector.

Despite dying young, Lenny Bruce was a trailblazer. Unfortunately, due to drug addiction, he died far too soon.

Bruce's short but amazing career paved the way for many comedians, especially Dick Gregory and Richard Pryor.

Lenny's Famous quotes and comments:

'In the halls of justice, the only justice is in the halls.'

'A lot of people say to me, 'Why did you kill Christ?' I dunno...it was one of those parties, got out of hand, you know. We killed him because he didn't want to become a doctor; that's why we killed him.'

'Every day, people are straying away from the church and going back to Gd.'

'Take away the right to say 'FUCK', and you take away the right to say, 'FUCK the Government'.'

'If Jesus had been killed 20 years ago, Catholic school children would be wearing little electric chairs around their necks instead of crosses.'

'I won't say ours was a tough school, but we had our own coroner. We used to write essays like: What I'm going to be if I grow up.'

Lenny talked a lot about school & religion. So, I have added a few old Jewish jokes on the subject:

Yeshiva (Jewish school of learning).

The first day, after the teacher finished the lesson, he asked if anyone had any questions. A young boy put his hand up and said, 'I've got one. According to you and the bible, the Children of Israel crossed the Red Sea, yes?'
'Yes, that's right.'
'And the Children of Israel defeated the Philistines and the Egyptians, and they built the Temple, and they were always doing something important, right?'
'Yes, that's all correct; what the question is?'
'Well, what were the grown-ups doing?'

There was this Jewish kid, not a well-behaved child. He went to the local Jewish school but was expelled for fighting and misbehaviour. His parents were not happy but raised the money and sent him to private school. But within six months, they wanted him out. They then sent him to the local Catholic school. He was six months in, and his parents were amazed he was still in school. 'Why, after three schools, Jewish, private and now public, are you now so settled?' He took them to the great hall and said, 'Hey, have you seen what they do to you if you misbehave! Look on the wall with the guy on the cross!'

Henry Churniavsky's insight into school

I attended private school, and I was always in trouble, always in detention, which was corporal punishment in this school. But I must say I was lucky as the year before I arrived, they had capital punishment!

I remember once; I was talking in art class. The teacher (an ex English Rugby International) picked me up with one hand by my jacket and hung me on a coat hook for the rest of the lesson. Big lesson learnt that day.

Peter Sellers 1925 - 1980

Peter Sellers (Richard Henry Sellers) was born in Southsea, Portsmouth. He is mainly remembered for some great films, including 'Dr Strangelove', 'The Pink Panther' films and 'Being There.' He also led a very colourful personal life.

His Yorkshire parents, William and Agnes 'Peg' Sellers were both variety and vaudeville entertainers. Peg was in the Ray Sisters troupe. William was Protestant while Peg was Jewish, and they pushed Peter at an early age onto the stage. In fact, Peter was only two weeks old when he was carried on stage by Dick Henderson. Touring played a large part in the Sellers' family life and did cause much upheaval in young Sellers' life. Peter maintained a very close relationship with his mother, to the extent he was indulged by his overprotective mother throughout her life. When Peter was small, he pushed his aunt into a lit fire, and his mother just laughed.

In 1939 his parents moved to Ilfracombe in Devon, and at 14, the then legal age to leave school ended Sellers education; he was now spending his days working in local theatres doing odd jobs, leaning to play drums and ukulele and then toured with the Entertainments National Service Association (ENSA). In 1943, at 18, he was called into the military service.

When Sellers was in the RAF, where he joined the RAF Entertainment Unit, he developed his mimicry and improvisational skills at a very early age in the 'Gang Shows' when he entertained troops in the UK and the Far East.

On Akyab Island, Burma, Sellers produced 35mm film reels. They showed various footage of his time on stage, playing the drums in a jazz quintet and acting in a two-handed sketch at only 19 years of age.

Radio followed after the war, and in the early 1950s came the Goon Show (with Harry Secombe and Spike Milligan), which ended in 1980.

The 1950s and 1960s were Sellers' heyday. He even mixed with royalty! He was a close friend of Princess Margaret and enjoyed her company. It is said that he had a crush on her. Princess Margaret even appeared in a home movie which Sellers made. Due to the many complexities that Sellers had in his life, her only comment on him was that, 'He was the most difficult man I ever knew'.

My father introduced me to 'The Goon Show' when I was a young boy, I was hooked, and I made my dad buy all the cassettes he could, so I could listen on my recorder late into the night.

Some of these recordings were with a live audience, and the last 'Goon Show' of all was a major success. His radio success led to solo comedy recordings (one with

Sophia Loren - *I only mention this as my dad had a huge crush on her!)*. These recordings were a source for the ideas of future artists such as 'Monty Python and The Bonzo Dog Band'.

Sellers used musical satire, and his early work was produced by an upcoming producer at the time, George Martin, who became The Beatles most celebrated producer.

Again, Sellers was not a stand-up per se, but his films and radio work were unique. He was, by many, considered a comic genius.

Peter's Famous quotes:

'Gentlemen, you can't fight in here. This is a war room.'

'There used to be a real me, but I had it surgically removed.'

'Finally, in conclusion, let me just say.'

'Contraceptives should be used on every conceivable occasion.'

Peter talked about surgery. So, I have added an old Jewish joke on the subject:

Sometimes people ask me, can I explain being Jewish. What does this mean? Let me give you this example. A man is about to have a life-threatening operation done by his son, one of the best surgeons in the country. He asks to see him just before the anaesthetic is given. 'Son, you do your best, but remember, if it goes wrong, your mother will be moving in with you and your new wife.'

Henry Churniavsky's insight into contraceptives

In my role as a medical representative, you hear all sorts from doctors, nurses and even patients. I remember a time when I was waiting to see a consultant (in a professional capacity this time!). Next to me was a young woman who was with her mother. A nurse had sat down next to them and was asking the young girl questions; you know, basic stuff, name, address, date of birth. The nurse then asked her, 'Do you now use, or have you ever used recreational drugs?'

The young girl blushed, much to the shock of her mum, and said, 'Yes, birth control pills.'

Shelley Berman 1925 – 2017

Sheldon Leonard Berman was born in Chicago in 1925. He was an outstanding American comedian, actor, writer, teacher, lecturer and poet. He spent over 20 years teaching humour. He also received three gold awards for his albums. He was the first to get a Grammy award for a spoken comedy recording.

Shelley was the son of Irene and Nathan Berman. Berman started his acting career after WW2. He had jobs such as driving a cab, and being a dancing instructor, while he was studying acting at HB Studios. He later found work as a sketch writer on 'The Steve Allen Plymouth Show'.

In the 1950s, Berman was in Chicago with 'The Compass Players', which evolved into 'The Second City'. While doing improv, he started some solo projects, one being on stage with an imaginary telephone.

By 1957 Berman had started his stand-up at 'Mister Kelly's' in Chicago, which got him noticed and got him more gigs and a recording contract. Broadway was another avenue for Berman with 'A Family Affair' and 'The Odd Couple', and more shows followed.

His albums sold well *(I remember my dad buying 'Inside Shelley Berman' & 'Outside Shelley Berman'; he recorded it onto a cassette which I would listen to, when I was eight or nine years old, in my room at night).*

He was a regular on TV shows, including 'What's My Line' in the 1960s. Berman wrote three books; he was also in films from 1955 – 2008, including 'Dementia', 'Meet the Fockers' and 'You Don't Mess with the Zohan'.

Berman was the first comedian to perform stand-up at Carnegie Hall, and Steve Martin thanked him by saying, 'Shelley Berman changed modern stand-up'.

Berman had an issue with fellow comedian Bob Newhart; he said that he had plagiarised his improv.

Shelley's Famous quotes:

'My whole act is confession.'

'The Steve Allen, Saturday Night Show, had the right to two options after my first performance.'

'Unquestionably, stand-up comedy is and has always been an art form.'

'A prominent L.A. psychiatrist told a patient, 'Ridiculous that you should still be frightened of thunder at your age. Thunder is a mere natural phenomenon. Now the next time it storms, and you hear a couple of claps of thunder, just do as I do, put your head under a pillow and stuff your ears until the thunder goes away.''

'I know a husband whose neighbour boasted, 'I got a cute little red sports car for my wife.'

'Gosh,' said my friend, 'I wish I could make a trade like that.''

Shelley talked about psychiatry. So, I have added old Jewish jokes on the subject:

Moshe goes to see his psychiatrist, 'Doctor, my wife Fay is being unfaithful to me. Every night, she goes to Keith's Wine Bar and picks up a man. She sleeps with anybody who asks her to. I'm going crazy with worry. What on earth should I do?'

'Relax,' says the doctor, 'Take a couple of deep breaths and try to calm down. Now, first of all, tell me exactly where Keith's Wine Bar is?'

Monty is having a session with his psychiatrist. Dr Cohen draws a picture of a triangle and asks Monty what it looks like to him. Monty, with excitement, says, 'It looks like a man and a woman in bed.'

'Mmmm', says the doctor.

He then draws another picture, this time a square, and asks the same question. Monty again looks excited and says, 'It looks like a man and a woman in bed.'

'Mmmm', says the doctor, a bit puzzled. He draws a circle and shows Monty.

Monty, a bit more agitated, says, 'It looks like a man and a woman having sex.'

Dr Cohen looks at Monty and says, 'Young man, I think you have too much sex on your mind.'

Monty replies, 'That's a bit rich coming from you; it's you who's drawing the dirty pictures.'

Sammy Davis Jr 1925 – 1990

Sammy Davis Jr (Samuel George Davis Jr.) was born in Harlem in 1925; he was an American singer, musician, dancer, actor and comedian. He was well known for his impressions of actors, musicians and celebrities.

Davis was the son of African American entertainer Sammy Davis Sr. His mother was a Cuban American tap dancer Elvera. Now Sammy was not Jewish. *(So why is he in the book, you may ask? Hang on, be patient, I will tell you).* In the late 1950s, he converted to Judaism. After many conversations with Eddie Cantor, he found a bond between the oppression of African Americans and the Jewish community. *(Now you know!)*

Davis Jr. started in show business aged three, in vaudeville, with his dad and the 'Will Mastin Trio' with whom he had a long partnership. After his military service came to an end, he returned to the Trio and then went on to perform at Ciro's in Hollywood in 1951.

In 1953 Davis was offered his own television show on ABC, but as they could not get a sponsor, it was dropped. It was not long, however, before his fame took off. In 1956, after singing the title song from 'Six Bridges to Cross', he starred on Broadway in the musical 'Mr Wonderful'.

In 1959 Davis became part of the 'Rat Pack', led by Frank Sinatra and included Dean Martin, Joey Bishop, and Peter Lawford. The Rat Pack made many films together, including 'Oceans 11' (1960), 'Sergeants 3' (1962), and 'Robin and the 7 Hoods' (1964); they also performed on stage in Las Vegas.

Davis went on to make records, talk shows and TV specials. In the late 1960s, he was a top-drawer act in Las Vegas along with his friend, Elvis Presley.

Sammy's Famous quotes,

'Alcohol gives you infinite patience for stupidity.'

'I have to be a star like another man has to breathe.'

'If you want to be the best, baby, you've got to work harder than anyone else.'

'You have to be able to look back at your life and say, 'Yeah, that was fun.''

'I had more clothes than I had closets, more cars than garage space, but no money.'

'You don't swing where you sleep.'

'You always have two choices: your commitment versus your fear.'

'The Jews are a swinging bunch of people. I mean, I've heard of persecution, but what they went through is ridiculous. But the great thing is, after thousands of years of waiting, and fighting, and holding on, they finally made it.'

1926

Don Rickles 1926 – 2017

Don Rickles was born in New York City in 1926. He was a stand-up comedian, actor and author. Don was the ultimate putdown artist, the master of insult. No one was safe, regardless of gender, ethnicity, sexual orientation or cultural standing. No one would escape 'Mr Warmth'.
Don was born to Jewish parents Max and Etta Rickles. Max was from Lithuania and Etta, Austria. He grew up in Jackson Heights.

Acting was his first choice of career, but early in his career, around 1948, he got frustrated by the lack of work, so he turned to comedy in New York, Miami and LA.

In the early 1950s, his comedy was taking off, and he even started calling his audience 'hockey pucks'. Rickles got lucky by getting some major celebrities on his side. It began at a gig in 1957, at Slate Bros in Hollywood; Frank Sinatra was there to watch the show. Rickles roasted him, and Sinatra loved it; he encouraged his friends and other celebrities to see Rickles and liked to watch him roast them.

Known as 'Merchant of Venom' and 'Mr Warmth', he made over 100 appearances on 'The Tonight Show', and his live comedy album got into the charts. Within two years, he was headlining in Las Vegas.

His first comedy album, in 1968, 'Hello Dummy', was a live recording that included a rant about his wife's sexual fetishes.

For the follow up in 1969, Don had a group of five panellists posing questions; Don was then ad-libbing answers.

Starting in 1974 and for over ten years till around 1984, Rickles was on the 'Dean Martin Celebrity Roast' specials which gained him more popularity.

In the 1980s, Rickles performed with Steve Lawrence in Las Vegas. One of his highlights was to perform at Ronald Reagan's second inauguration.

He continued his stand-up into the 1980s in Atlantic City at the Tropicana Hotel and Casino. In 1993 Rickles co-starred with Richard Lewis in 'Daddy Dearest', but this was short-lived.

Don's Famous quotes:

'Who picks your clothes? Stevie Wonder.'

'Show business is my life. When I was a kid, I sold insurance, but nobody laughed.'

On Frank Sinatra: 'When you enter a room, you have to kiss his ring. I don't mind, but he has it in his back pocket.'

'Some people say funny things, but I say things funny.'

Henry Churniavsky's insight into funny things at work

I've been on loads of Personality Presentation Courses, or as I call them, Sales Prevention Courses. They get you to fill out answers to questions, and the result gives you a colour which means the type of person you are. You can be red, green, yellow or blue. It's to see who you are most compatible with. To be honest, if I look at a woman, I know if we are going to be compatible, fuck the colours! I've studied this for years, and I know if I look at a woman and I say, 'I know we are opposite despite whatever colour you are, you see I know I would have sex with you, but I know you won't with me.'

I did another test recently. The results said I was a shallow thinker and naïve. FFS, they have just described me as Homer Simpson.

I was once asked in an interview what was my main weakness; I hate that question. I said, 'It would be my issues with reality, but my main strength is, I am Spiderman.'

Shecky Greene 1926 –

Shecky Greene (Fred Sheldon Greenfield) was born on the North Side of Chicago in 1926. He is an American comedian, best known for his nightclub performances in Las Vegas, where he became a headliner in the 1950s.

Greene served in the United States Navy during World War II, but comedy was his love, and in the early days, he performed in New Orleans, where he stayed for six years. He moved on to gigs in Miami, Chicago and Lake Tahoe until he was persuaded in 1954 to move to Las Vegas. It is said Greene introduced Elvis to Las Vegas.

1953 was the turning point for Greene; he was signed to the Chez Paree in Chicago as an opening act for Ann Sothern, while his counterparts, Joe E Lewis and Sophie Tucker, were doing well in Nevada. It was then that the Golden Hotel, Reno offered Green £1,000 a week for a four-week stint. After one performance, the owners renegotiated a new deal worth $20,000 a month.

In 1975 the MGM Grand Hotel opened with Dean Martin as the headline act. Greene was the second headline act, and at one point, he was earning $150,000 a week. Greene was a massive horse racing fan and joked that 'despite earning $150,000 a week, $125,000 went to his bookmaker.'

Greene played 'Carnegie Hall' and appeared on 'The Ed Sullivan Show', 'The Merv Griffin Show', 'The Mike Douglas Show', and Johnny Carson was a big fan. He made over 40 appearances on 'The Tonight Show'. Greene has won many awards, including 'Best Lounge Entertainer', The Jimmy Durante award for 'Best Comedian.' And 'Male Comedy Star'.

One of his standard jokes was, 'Johnny was a good boy, never smoked, never drank, never dated. On his graduation day from college, his parents asked what he wanted. Johnny replied, 'A drunken broad that smokes."

Shecky's Famous Quotes:

'I have a daughter who goes to SMU. She could've gone to UCLA here in California, but it's one more letter she'd have to remember.'

On Frank Sinatra: 'Frank saved my life once. He said, 'Okay, boys. That's enough."

1926 - 1930

Mike and Bernie Winters (Mike 1926 - 2013) (Bernie 1930 – 1991)

Mike and Bernie were brothers born in Islington, London. They performed a music and comedy double act with the aid of their St. Bernard dog, Schnorbitz. They were a very popular act from the mid-1950s to the early 1970s.

Despite living in the shadow of Morecambe and Wise, the Winter Brothers were part of the golden age of British TV.

One of their grandfathers arrived from Russia, aged 16 and ran a restaurant in Whitechapel. The Winter brothers' father, Samuel, was a boxer and gambler. Their mother, Rachel, came from a circus family. In fact, Rachel's brothers were champion boxers Jack Bloomfield and Joe Bloomfield.

The brothers at the beginning had a very musical background. Mike studied at the Royal Academy of Music, playing the clarinet. Bernie, who was self-taught, played the ukulele and performed as a comedian. After WWII, they joined forces doing a double act playing musical items and doing impressions.

Not long after their discharge, they won a talent competition in Manchester. The first prize was a tour of variety theatres. Success did not follow, and it led to them splitting up, only later forming a three-handed act, 'The Three Loose Screws', where they added dancing to their repertoire. In 1955 Mike and Bernie made their first appearance on the BBC's 'Variety Parade', and they stayed till 1958.

Their big break came on ITV's 'Sunday Night at the Palladium', and they performed together for another 20 years before ending their partnership in 1978.

In the 1980s, Mike moved to Florida and eventually opened, with boxing manager, Angelo Dundee, a theatre club in Miami.

Bernie continued with 'Schnorbitz' and also hosted quiz shows. Bernie died in 1991. Mike returned to the UK and died in 2013, aged 86.

Catchphrase: Bernie had a unique way of talking to his brother, who he referred to as 'Coochie-face', and he would say to him, 'I'll smash yer face in.'

Jerry Lewis 1926 – 2017

Jerry Lewis (Joseph Levitch) was born in Newark, New Jersey, in 1926. Lewis was an all-round entertainer, comedian, actor, singer and filmmaker. He was dubbed 'The King of Comedy' and 'The Total Filmmaker'.

Jerry's father, Danie, 'Danny' Levitch, was a master of ceremonies, and vaudevillian, who performed under the name of Danny Lewis. His mother, Rachael 'Rae' Levitch, was a WOR (radio station) pianist and was also Danny's music director. Both had come from Russia.

Jerry Lewis had his stage debut at five, and by his mid-teens was a professional comedian. At 15, he had an act miming lyrics from songs; he landed a gig at the Burlesque House in Buffalo, but it wasn't successful, and no more shows were booked. However, veteran burlesque comedian Max Coleman, and Irving Kaye, a Borscht Belt comedian (who became his manager), helped him get future Borscht Belt appearances.

Gaining some attention, he started a double act with another star in the making, Dean Martin. They were a great comedy act, but what separated them from other acts was their ability to add ad-libbed segments into their routines. The duo started to work together at the '500 Club' in Atlantic City in 1946, which saw them rise to national prominence doing their popular nightclub act. They also starred on NBC Radio.

Two live TV performances in 1959 resulted in them being signed to NBC for weekly radio shows. Films followed for the two of them, fourteen in total between 1950-1956. Their styles complemented each other; Martin was the suave, sophisticated half, while Lewis was full of physical energy.

In 1956 an acrimonious split saw Lewis at a crossroads in his life; he was asked to fill in for a show in Las Vegas, in which he sang, and he said, these are his in his own words; 'I walked off stage knowing I could make it on my own.'

Music and films followed for Jerry Lewis, and he was a major success performing on many stages.
He had regular spots at the Sands Hotel and Casino and shows in Miami, New York, Chicago and Washington.

TV spots were now happening for him as a solo artist, and he even had to ad lib a 20-minute spot at the 31st Academy Awards in 1959 due to the show being 20 minutes short.

Comedy films followed, such as 'The Delicate Delinquent', which was the first film he produced.
He was now the highest-paid person in Hollywood, which gave him unlimited creative control.

In 1962 he was a guest host on 'The Tonight Show'; this showing had the highest ratings for years.

The 1970s showed no let-up; with many guest appearances, he produced scripts and directed films.

In 1976 on the Jerry Lewis MDA Telethon, Frank Sinatra brought Dean Martin on stage, where they embraced. It was seen as one of the iconic moments in history, and it looked like all the bad blood between them evaporated.

In 1983 Lewis starred in Martin Scorsese's film, 'The King of Comedy.' Lewis's last appearance was on TV was in 2016, 'Comedians in Cars Getting Coffee.'

Jerry's Famous quotes:

'I've had a great success being a total idiot.'

'My ego and my vanities have nothing to do with comedy.'

'When you walk in front of an audience, they are the kings and queens.'

Henry Churniavsky's insight into audiences (foreign).

One of the hardest things to do is to do comedy at a foreign corporate gig. Especially if some of the audience don't speak English. I did one recently; 50% of the audience had to wear headphones, and an interpreter translated my stuff. I started and got a few laughs, and then a few seconds later, the Italians in unison laughed really loud. I told another joke, and again laughter from the English followed by a really loud laugh. I finished the set with the same outcome on each joke. At the end, I asked the interpreter, 'Was it easy to translate my Jokes?' He replied, 'Not really; I just told them you were an English comic telling a joke, and when you stopped, they should laugh out loud.'

Mel Brooks 1926 –

Mel Brooks (Melvin Kaminsky) was born in Brooklyn, New York, in 1926. He was an American director, writer, actor, comedian, composer and show producer. Mel's parents were Max and Kate Kaminsky; he was the youngest of four boys, and he grew up in Williamsburg. His father's family were from Germany, and his mother was from Kiev. Unfortunately, Brooks' father died at 34 when Mel was only two. At nine years old, he decided, after seeing a Broadway show, that he was going to go into show business and not the garment business.

In 1942, at 14 years old, he was a pool 'tummler.' At this age, he also taught Buddy Rich to play the drums, and Brooks was also earning money in the Catskills as a musician. At 16, due to an illness with a regular MC, Brooks stepped in and was given his chance as a comedian, still under the name of Melvin Kaminsky, due to his comedic antics around the camp. After this became a master 'tummler' entertainer at Grossinger's Hotel in the Borscht Belt.

He was drafted into the army in 1944; he took part in organising shows for the troops.
In 1949 Sid Caesar hired Brooks to become his joke writer.

The 1950s saw a variety of comedy shows which included Brooks, Carl Reiner, Neil Simon and others, including, later, Woody Allen.

Brooks and Reiner became close friends and would improvise comedy routines when they were not working. Reiner always played the straight man to Brooks' many different characters. Then a new character emerged, a 2,000 year-old-man. By the late 1950s, they were performing this routine in New York City.

In 1960 Brooks moved to Hollywood, where he began creating Broadway musicals, short films and TV programmes like 'Get Smart'.

Brooks was now moving in different circles. By 1967 he was ready to give the world films such as 'The Producers', 'Blazing Saddles', 'Young Frankenstein', 'Robin Hood: Men in Tights' and 'High Anxiety' (*I mention his films as they are still some of my favourite comedy films ever*). Many more films followed.

During the 1970s, Brooks had also produced a Robin Hood parody for TV.
In 1983 'An Audience with Mel Brooks' was another triumph. It was a chance to display his wit to a live audience.

Since 2005 some of his films have been turned into musicals including, 'The Producers', 'Young

Frankenstein', and it is possible that 'Blazing Saddles' may follow.

Brooks is only one of a handful of people to receive an Oscar, a Tony and a Grammy.

In 2015 Brooks did 'Live at the Geffen' – a stand-up special.

Mel's Famous quotes:

'Being old is getting up in the middle of the night, as often as George Clooney, but not for the same reason.'

'Tragedy is when I cut my finger. Comedy is when you walk into an open sewer and die.'

'Bad taste is simply saying the truth before it should be said.'

'If presidents can't do it to their wives, they do it to their country.'

'Oh, I'm not a true genius. I'm a near-genius. I would say I'm a short genius. I'd rather be tall and normal than a short genius.'

'If Gd wanted us to fly, He would have given us tickets.'

Henry Churniavsky's insight into getting up in the night

You know, as you get older, you wake up more during the night and have to go to the toilet more often. Being at home, that's not an issue. I know with my eyes closed how to get to the toilet and back without waking the other half. However, holidays can be more problematic.

A few years ago we rented a villa in Lanzarote and on the first night I woke up. I carefully left the room (my eyes not fully open but squinting) and entered another. Luckily the light came on automatically; I did my business, and as I left, the light went out, and I climbed back into bed. The wife was still snoring, and I fell asleep for the rest of the night.

In the morning, my wife woke and said, 'Did you sleep ok?'

'Yes, I did, I only got up once, and I did not wake you up either.'

My wife smiled and left the room. A few seconds later, she screamed, 'For Gd's sake, you pissed in the fridge.'

Henry Churniavsky's insight into flying/getting into America

Have you ever travelled to America? You have to fill out what they call an ESTA form (Electronic System for Travel Authorisation). This has taken over from the visa you used to need.

My daughter's father-in-law was filling out the ESTA for himself and his wife. Now, do you know the 3rd

question? It is, 'Do you seek to engage, or have you ever engaged, in terrorist activities, espionage, sabotage or genocide?' In my humble opinion, it's an easy question to answer; it's a yes or no answer. In fact, 'No' is already ticked, so if you want to change the answer, you have to click no first! Well, my daughter's father-in-law, 'by mistake' he says, ticked 'Yes', so of course his wife was barred from entry. Now I know he does not like her, and he wanted a trip on his own, but really! She eventually had to go to the American embassy, and she did get a full visa in the end after some explaining.

It got me thinking, how would this question affect an actual terrorist? We know Donald Trump wants to be strong against terrorism, but will this help?

Can you picture a terrorist filling out the form, 'Well, I want to bomb the infidel, but do I lie?' Maybe we need an extra question...do you wish to book a return flight, or is this one way!

1927

Alan King 1927 – 2004

Alan King (Irwin Alan Kniberg) was born in New York City in 1927. King was an American actor and comedian. He was well known for his rants and biting wit. He was known as a Jewish comedian and satirist.

At 14, King performed on the radio in a competition; although he did not win, he was invited to join a nationwide tour. At 15, he was performing comedy at the Hotel Gradus, where else than in the Catskill Mountains. This did not last long as he made a joke on stage about the hotel owner and was fired, but he became an MC in the New Prospect Hotel in New York. Work took him to a Canadian burlesque house when he followed his other passion, boxing.

King started his comedy career as a one-liner comedian, and he focused on mother-in-law jokes and Jews. Later he changed to a more conversational comedy, using everyday life as his new focus, and this was more accepted. This style inspired other comics including, Joan Rivers, Jerry Seinfeld, Larry David, Billy Crystal and Bill Cosby *(sorry for the mention)*.

In the late 1940s King moved to Long Island and again redeveloped his comedy to include suburbia.

He was now opening for some big celebrities such as Judy Garland, Nat King Cole, Lena Horne and Tony Martin.

He ventured into films in the 1950s and worked in the film industry up until 1995, playing a variety of roles.

Like many other Jewish comics of this era, King worked the Catskill circuit, but his career took off when he got onto The Ed Sullivan Show and other shows of the time. Because he based himself just outside New York City, he was often available when an act needed filling if anyone had to cancel at short notice.

In 1972 he hosted the Oscars and was MC for President John F. Kennedy's inauguration in 1961.
King was a long-standing host of the 'New York Friars Club Celebrity Roasts' and was well respected within the industry.

Alan's Famous quotes:

'When I was in hospital, they gave me apple juice every morning, even after I told them I didn't like it. I had to get even. One morning, I poured the apple juice into the specimen tube. The nurse held it up and said, 'It's a little cloudy.' I took the tube from her and said, 'Let me run it through again, and drank it. The nurse fainted.''

'A summary of every Jewish holiday: They tried to kill us, we won, let's eat.'

'Did you hear the one about the elderly Jew on his deathbed who sent for a priest, after declaring to his astonished relatives that, 'I want to convert?' Asked why he would become a Catholic, after living all his life a Jew, he answered, 'Better one of them should die than one of us.'

'You do live longer with bran, but you spend the last 15 years on the toilet.'

'As a parent, I'd – I'd be a better father.'

'When I read Dickens for the first time, I thought he was Jewish because he wrote about oppression, and bigotry, all the things that my father talked about.'

'When you're my age, you worry about two things. One is when a woman says, 'Let's do it again, right now,' and the other is, who's going to come to my funeral.''

'My father helped me leave. He said, 'It's all out there; it's not here.''

King also wrote a number of books, the last being in 2005 – Matzoh Balls for Breakfast: and Other Memories of Growing up Jewish.

Alan talked a lot about death/funerals. So, I have added a couple of old Jewish jokes on the subject:

An old Jewish man was on his deathbed, and he shouts, 'Sarah, Sarah, where is my wonderful wife?' 'I am here, darling, by your bedside; I am not leaving you, we have been married for over 50 years, and now I should leave your side?'
'Simon, Simon, where is my favourite son who I depend on?'
'I am here, Papa, by your side, where else.'
'Rachel, Rachel, my unmarried, too fussy princess daughter, the light of my life, where are you?' 'Papa, Papa, I am here right next to mama, don't worry, I am here.'
'You are all here! So, who is looking after the shop?'

The dutiful Jewish son is sitting at his father's bedside. His father is near death.
Father: "Son."
Son: "Yes, Dad."
Father: (weakly) "Son. That smell. Is your mother making my favourite cheesecake?"
Son: "Yes, Dad"
Father: (even weaker) "Ah, if I could just have one more piece of your mom's cheesecake. Would you get me a piece, please?"
Son: "Ok, Dad. (The son leaves and goes to the kitchen. He returns and sits next to his father)
Father: "Is that you, son?"

Son: Yes, Dad."

Father: "Did you bring me the cheesecake I so desperately want to taste before I die?"

Son: "No, Dad."

Father: "Why? It's my dying wish!"

Son: "Well, Dad. Mom says the cake is for after the funeral."

Henry Churniavsky's insight into a Jewish Holiday: Yom Kippur:

We know the Jewish people are the chosen race; it's in our bible! I will explain to our friends of a different faith.

What is the most important thing to humans - food? Now, food is so important to us Jews. Let me explain why Gd has chosen the Jewish religion. For example, Muslims have Ramadan. A fast which they have to starve all day for a month. Really, a month of not eating during the day!

Christians have Lent - again, a month of fasting of one item you like the most. Apparently, you can't give up something you don't like!

Now, what do the Jewish people have to do for fasting? Yom Kippur. One day, yes, one day we fast for 24 hours, that's all, no month for us Jews. Gd knows we could not last a month. A month with no food or even a favourite food. And to make sure we can cope we have a big meal the night before the fast starts (starts early evening) and an even bigger one right after it finishes. We also stock up the week before with our two-day New Year celebrations. Yes, Gd has looked after us.

Henry Churniavsky's insight into growing up Jewish and his memories:

THE EARLY YEARS with MUM

I always had a weight problem, not my fault. My nickname was 'Fat Bastard', but you know mothers can be so cruel. My weight issue is not my fault; it is down to my Mum. I inherited that 'obese gene' everyone talks about now. It can only be described as a hyperactive knife and fork.

I've recently read that obesity is more dangerous than smoking cigarettes - does that now mean I have to eat all my meals outside at restaurants?

My mother did not know the basics of diet for kids, especially as I was the firstborn. She would crush three Farley's Rusks into a bottle with full-fat milk (the 1960s had no concept of semi-skimmed milk). She would heat this up and have to cut the top of the teat off, so the rusks would come out; she gave this to me **3 TIMES A DAY,** in between meals.

One day after kindergarten, I came home, and the first person I saw was my dad. 'Dad, I got a part in the school play.'
'Great, what part?' he asked.

I replied, 'Oh, I'm playing a married Jewish man of 25 years.'

'Never mind, son,' my Dad said, 'let's hope next year you get a speaking part.'

Aged six, one night at home, I was doing homework in my bedroom. I turned to my Mum and said, 'Mum, do you know what UFO stands for?'

My Mum looked at me in admiration, 'No son, what it stands for?'

'U F**K OFF!'

WHACK!! My Mum hit me so hard around the head that I fell off the bed.

Mum looked at me. 'Now, what have you to say for yourself?'

I looked at her and said, 'F**k all now.'

I remember when I was young, I was rushed to Hospital A&E with a very high temperature and vomiting. The doctor carried out some tests and then asked me what bothered me the most. Apparently, I looked at him and said, 'I would have to say, my sisters.'

My Mum was always tired. It's hard with three kids at home. But she always had a cunning plan. Each day at 5 pm, my Mum would go into the living room and put the clock to 6 pm and call us in and show us it was time for bed. There was no moaning or arguing, not with the stare my Mum could give you. We were frogmarched upstairs, washed and in bed by, in real terms, 5.30 pm. She would *then come downstairs and alter the clock back to the right time, and at the latest, we would be in bed by 6.30 pm. It took me until I was 18 to realise there was a 6 o'clock news programme.*

Mort Sahl 1927 - 2021

Mort Sahl (Morton Lyon Sahl) was born in Montreal, Canada, in 1927. His family relocated to Los Angeles.

He was an American comedian, actor and provocative political satirist and considered to be the first modern stand-up comedian. He, arguably, was the most influential comedian of the popular era. Between 1950 - 53 Sahl tried to get jobs as a stand-up comedian in over 30 nightclubs in Los Angeles with no success. People told him he would never make it. Undeterred, he and a friend rented an old theatre to try his luck, but again, it failed to take off as the audiences were not big enough to sustain it.

Sahl then tried to change his act to incorporate the short stories he had written and tried to use them as a monologue, but this failed as well. He moved to San Francisco for the love of a woman, and there he eventually got a break. The owner of Hungry I, Enrico Banducci, saw something in Sahl's act and offered him his first full-time spot as a stand-up comedian.

Sahl's satirical comedy started to go well. Other major comics came to see him, including Danny Kaye and Eddie Cantor, who even gave him help and advice. The advice really helped, and at the end of the first year at Hungry I, Sahl had gone from his starting salary of $75 per week to $3,000.

Sahl now started to spread his wings and performed in Chicago, Los Angeles and New York. What was unique to Sahl, at the time, as a stand-up comedian, was that he had to be funny.

At the time, many of these clubs had never had this kind of act, so he was a trailblazer for future comedians. Woody Allen called him, 'A genius…who revolutionised the medium.' When John Cleese saw Sahl, he placed him on the same level as The Beatles and Elvis.

On TV, he was different to other comics. Comedians of that day used to appear on stage formal, in a suit, and well-rehearsed. Sahl was different; he would turn up in a V neck sweater and appear to be unrehearsed, which gave him this cool image.

Sahl's casual style influenced many comics of the time, like Lenny Bruce and Dick Gregory, but the difference was that he was less confrontational and focused on the day's politics. Woody Allen only decided to go into comedy after he saw Sahl perform and talk about his personal life.

It is said that in the 1950s, Mort Sahl re-invented stand-up comedy. In 1956 he made his debut on NBC Comedy Hour.

His knack for staying current and getting material from the day's newspapers kept his comedy fresh. In 1960 he was a Time magazine cover story, and he was the first comic to make a record album, the first to do college concerts and the first to win a Grammy.

His friends included high political leaders; John F Kennedy asked him for a list of jokes he could use.

In 1963 after Kennedy's assassination, Sahl's comedy started to reflect his politics, which in certain areas did not go down well. His obsession with Kennedy seemed to wreck his career.

In the 1970s, there was a rise in 'counterculture', which gave Sahl a new lease of life. A comeback followed as a veteran comedian, and he was now included in a set of new and upcoming comedians, including George Carlin, Lily Tomlin and Richard Prior.

The 1980s had Sahl back headlining at Banducci's new clubs in San Francisco, and in 1987 he had a successful tour in Australia.

1988 saw Sahl back in New York to perform Off-Broadway in a one-man show, 'Mort Sahl's America', which got great reviews - but it was not a box office success.

He was still performing in the 1990s in theatres and colleges, and he appeared in New York again in 2001.

Sahl, now 92, still performs every Thursday live in California.

He was voted No.40 in a top 100 stand-up comics of all time by Comedy Central.

Sahl never swore on or off stage. Milton Berle described him as 'One of the greatest political satirists of all time'. He had a unique stage presence; wearing his trademark V neck sweater, he would often come on stage with a newspaper and would talk about events, people in the news or the paper and relate to his own stories.

Mort's Famous quotes:

'The bravest thing that men do is love women.'

'A conservative is someone who believes in reform. But not now.'

'Washington couldn't lie. Nixon couldn't tell the truth, and Reagan couldn't tell the difference.'

'People tell me there are a lot of guys like me, which does not explain why I'm lonely.'

'Liberals feel unworthy of their possessions. Conservatives feel they deserve everything they've stolen.'

'My humour was Victorian...and still is.'

'Comedians have to challenge the power. Comedians should be dangerous and devastating, and funny. That's the hardest part.'

'Women have everything they want, and they've never been so unhappy.'

Henry Churniavsky's insight into women

I have now been married for over 30 years. I think now I am just starting to understand women (well, I say women, I really mean my wife), but you never really understand women. Over the years, there are things she has said which are not always what she means. When you get married, there is no rule book you can buy - like when your children eventually leave home to go to University, leaving the two of you alone in the house - where is the book; 'How to speak to your partner once the kids leave'. What the hell do you talk about?

Well, I decided before my son-in-law married my daughter that he may need some help. I made him a framed guide on the meaning of words a wife will use and what she means: please see below:

IT'S YOUR DECISION - NO, IT'S NOT.
WE NEED TO TALK - YOU NEED TO LISTEN AS SHE NEEDS TO COMPLAIN
YOU'RE VERY ATTENTIVE - IS SEX ALL YOU THINK ABOUT?

I'M SORRY - YOU WILL BE SORRY

YOU NEED TO LEARN HOW TO COMMUNICATE - JUST AGREE WITH HER AT ALL TIMES

I'M NOT UPSET - OH YES, SHE IS

DO YOU LOVE ME? - SHE WANTS SOMETHING

HOW MUCH DO YOU LOVE ME? – THIS IS DIFFERENT FROM ABOVE - SHE HAS DONE SOMETHING STUPID, AND YOU ARE NOT GOING TO LIKE IT.

I also gave him five deadly terms used by a wife to help him.

1. FINE - A wife uses this word to end an argument, and now is the time to shut up.
2. NOTHING - It means something, and you should be worried.
3. GO AHEAD - This is a dare, not permission (permission you need in triplicate, or at least in writing) - don't do it.
4. WHATEVER - A wife's way of saying 'Screw you'.
5. THAT'S OK - She is thinking, long and hard on how you will pay for that mistake

Bonus term:

6. WOW! - This is not to be taken as a compliment, but as amazement that you can be that stupid.

I have realised, as a married man, that the hardest dilemma facing me is when my wife says to me, 'You choose?' I just know whatever choice I make, I will be wrong!

Will Jordan 1927 - 2018

Will Jordan (born Wilbur Rauch) was born in the Bronx in 1927. An American character actor and stand-up comedian, best known for his resemblance to, and his impressions of, Ed Sullivan. Jordan grew up in Flushing, Queens, his father was a pharmacist, and his mother owned a hat store.

Jordan was a master at his craft. His best-known impression was of Ed Sullivan, who was a massive television personality. However, Sullivan had no real mannerisms to copy, making him hard to impersonate. Jordan invented some mannerisms such as cracking his knuckles, spinning and shaking back and forth. Jordan came up with the catchphrase 'Welcome to our Toast of the Town Shoooo' (later used as 'really big Shooo'), which was copied by nearly all Sullivan impersonators after him. In fact, he commented on this during an interview, 'The people that stole from me didn't need to,' he said, referring to other comedians who did Sullivan impressions. 'Jackie Mason, why would he need to steal from me? Jack Carter? Why would he steal from me?' he added. 'They weren't stealing from Ed. They were stealing my impression of Ed Sullivan.'

From 1970 Jordan portrayed Sullivan in films and in The Beatles film, 'I Wanna Hold Your Hand''. Jordan also appeared as Ed Sullivan on Billy Joel's hit 'Tell Her About

It'. Jordan appeared as Sullivan on Broadway in 'Bye Bye Birdie'.

Jordan did a number of impressions, which included Bing Crosby, Groucho Marx, Peter Lorre, James Mason and Jack Benny.

Jerry Stiller 1927 - 2020

Jerry Stiller (born Gerald Issac Stiller) was an American comedian-actor. For many years, he was part of a comedy team with his wife Anne Meara - Stiller and Meara. Stiller appeared in sitcoms such as 'Seinfeld' and 'The King of Queens'. Fun fact – Stiller and Meara are the parents of Ben Stiller.

Jerry was the eldest of four children to Bella and William Stiller, a bus driver. Bella was born in Poland. After returning from World War II, serving in the U.S. Army, Stiller went to University and in 1950 obtained a degree in Speech and Drama. In 1953 Stiller met another comedian Anne Meara, and they married a year later. They became a comedy duo and joined the Chicago improvisational company 'The Compass Players'. By 1961 they were performing in nightclubs in New York.

Their act continued into the 60s and 70s, and they performed on variety shows on television, mainly The Ed Sullivan Show. When their variety act ran its course, they switched and had a successful career in radio commercials. They also had their own five-minute sketch comedy show, 'Take Five with Stiller and Meara', which ran from 1977-78.

Later, they were on HBO doing 'Sneak Previews' 1979-82; they also produced a sitcom, 'The Stiller and Meara Show'.

"Seinfeld" saw Stiller nominated for an Emmy, and he won the American Comedy Award for Funniest Male Guest Appearance.

Stiller has worked in commercials, and films, including 'Zoolander', 'Airport 1975', 'Hairspray', and in 2010 Stiller and Meara began a Yahoo web series discussing current topics. He has also published a memoir.

Jerry's Famous quotes:

The couple performed as Hershey Horowitz and Mary Elizabeth Doyle. One sketch began with Mary starting: 'They're having a dance tonight at my sodality.'
Hershey (Stiller): 'At your what?'
Mary: 'My sodality.'
Hershey: 'What's that?'
Mary: 'Well, it's a girls' organisation in my parish.'
Hershey: 'You mean like Hadassah?'
Mary: 'What's that?'
Hershey: 'It's a girls' organisation in my parish.'

'It can make you sad to look at pictures from your youth. So, there's a trick to it. The trick is not to look at later pictures.'

'I don't think my judgment is that good. I don't know what is funny.'

'We managed to hang in there. Today when people get married, there's a tendency to run away when things get tough. There is a lot of strength in hanging together.'

'During the Great Depression, when people laughed, their worries disappeared. Audiences loved these funny men. I decided to become one.'

'Creative comedy is like growing geraniums in a minefield.'

'Hollywood never knew there was a Vietnam War until they made the movie.'

Norm Crosby 1927 – 2020

Norman Lawrence Crosby was an American comedian born in Boston, Massachusetts. He was often referred to as 'The Master of Malaprop.'

Born to a Jewish family, he was the son of Ann and John Crosby, and he was raised in Dorchester, Boston.

When he started his solo career, in the 1950s, as a stand-up, he adopted a friendly, blue-collar guy next door approach. His monologues included many malapropisms. In 1964 he appeared on The 'Tonight Show, Starring Johnny Carson' and in 1968, he had a 12 week series on NBC where he co-starred on 'The Beautiful Phyllis Diller Show'.

By 1974 he co-hosted a variety series 'Everything Goes', and he was on many Dean Martin Roasts. From 1978 to 1981, he hosted a nationally syndicated series, which was a mix of up and coming comedians and vaudeville legends.

In 1983 he co-hosted the annual 'Jerry Lewis MDA Labor Day Telethon'.

Norm's Famous Quotes:

'When you go to court, you are putting your fate into the hands of twelve people who weren't smart enough to get out of jury duty.'

'If your eyes hurt after you drink coffee, you have to take the spoon out of the cup.'

'Why do Canadians like to do it doggie style? So they can both keep watching the hockey game.'

'All's fair if you have a really good attorney.'

'Listen to the blabbing brook.'

'When my dad was explaining the facts of life to me, he drew me a big diaphragm.'

'My school was so tough the school newspaper had an obituary section.'

Henry Churniavsky's insight into malaprops (all from my daughter)

My daughter is amazing. Just like her twin brother, they are both high flying solicitors. This fact does not deter her from giving me comedy gold with her malapropisms, for example:

'Stop calling the kettle black.'
'I hate that Battenburg cake. I hate Parmesan.'
'Don't pull the roof over my eyes.'
'Early bird catches the dawn.'
'Pulled her back in.'
'Words are bigger than actions.'
'Is Ash Wednesday, Bonfire Night?'

On a card to one of her best friends, she wrote, 'Love you to the earth and back.' I think she meant the moon.

When she came home one day soaking wet, she told us all, 'Look at me, I'm like a drowned rabbit.' (Drowned rat).

On helping me at a trade fair, selling, she meant to say, 'See, I can sell ice to the Eskimos', she actually said, 'I can sell shit of a horse.'

On a trip home on the train, I was drinking a coffee, and I received a call from my daughter. 'Dad, what's your STD?' I first had to apologise to the lady in front of me as I spat some of my coffee out, then I wondered how my daughter found out?

I asked her, 'Darling, what did you say?' She replied, 'Your STD...what time are you arriving home?' I was delighted to tell her it was ETA.

Do you know what a liquid lunch is? My daughter thinks it's SOUP!

1928

Bette Walker 1928 – 1982

Betty Walker (Born Edith Seeman) was born in New Jersey, in 1928, to Latvian Jewish immigrants. She was a Jewish-American actor and comedian, who's main performances were in the 1950s and 1960s.

At 21, she starred in a sitcom 'The Goldbergs' as a loud-mouthed, nosy neighbour. She also performed in a number of plays and television dramas.

As a comedian, she was best known for her 'telephone act'. She had a very pronounced nasal Yiddish accent that what we 'Jews' would call 'A Yenta.' Her best routines 'Call from Long Island', 'You don't have to be Jewish' and 'The Yiddish are Coming, The Yiddish are Coming.'

She delivered a monologue to her unseen friend 'Ceil'. She brought this Jewish act to a broader audience showing the Jewish stereotype of the 'overbearing mother'.

She appeared on 'The Tonight Show with Johnny Carson', 'The Merv Griffin Show', 'The Mike Douglas Show' and 'The Steve Allen Show' where she would usually do her call to 'Ceil'.

Walker released/performed on many comedy albums of the time, 'From Love and Laughter' (1960) to 'Aunt Lena and Her Entire Family Circle' (1979).

From a personal viewpoint, Bette Walker and a great team of comics got me into comedy when I was very young. My dad taped a recording of 'You don't have to be Jewish' (1965); I was six years old when I first listened to this album. Over the years, I forgot about this, and a few years ago, I was given a CD to play. I was driving to London and decided to put this CD on to listen to it. I was amazed, it was the one my dad played to me at six years old, and I knew every line. Thank you, Mr Neville Fox.

Walker received the honour of 'Queen of Comedy' along with Jean Carroll, Totie Fields & Belle Barth in a stand-up showcase called 'The J.A.P. Show: Jewish American Princesses of Comedy'.

Bette's Famous Quote:

'My husband forgot my birthday and my anniversary. I didn't feel bad. On the contrary, give me a guilty husband any day. Some of my best outfits came from guilt!'

Henry Churniavsky's insight into guilt (from his mother)

I rang my mum the other day, and this is what I mean:
Me: 'Morning, Mum, how are you?'

Mum: 'Who is this?'

Me: 'Mum, stop it, it's your one and only son.'

Mum: 'It can't be; he never rings.' **GUILT NO 1.**

Me: 'Okay, Mum, yes, it's me, stop being ridiculous. How are you?'

Mum: 'I've not eaten in a week?'

Me: 'For Gd's sake, Mum, why haven't you eaten anything?'

Mum: 'Because I did not want to have my mouth full in case you rang.' **GUILT NO 2.**

I recently installed an answerphone and advised her how to programme it; she wanted to do it her way, so I left her with it, and the next day I tried to call her. The phone went to the answerphone, and it clicked, and this is what I got.

'If you are a salesperson, press 1, a friend, press 2. If it's my son, who never calls, dial 999 because the shock will probably give me a heart attack.' **GUILT NO 3.**

Jackie Mason 1928 - 2021

Jackie Mason (Yacov Moshe Maza) was born in Sheboygan, Wisconsin, in 1928. Jackie Mason started stand-up late in life *(not as late as me! I was in my mid-50s! sorry, I digress).* The main reason was that he came from a long line of Rabbis. His father and brothers were all Rabbis. He became a Rabbi at 25, and when his father passed away, he decided to become a comedian. He once remarked, 'Somebody in the family had to make a living.'

He had a blend of self-deprecating humility with abrasive arrogance to highlight differences between Jewish and Gentile culture.

Mason wrote most of his own material, and he spoke about the importance of life. 'Money is not important; love is important. Fortunately, I love money.'

In 1955 Mason made his debut at the Fieldston Hotel in Swan Lake, New York. It was not a success; management considered his comedy was too far ahead of its time. A few years later, his humour was a hit in the Borscht Belt in New York. Nightclub performances followed, and then in 1962, he appeared on the 'Ed Sullivan Show' where he became a hit. However, in 1964 an infamous incident happened on the show were Ed Sullivan took offence to Mason giving him the one-finger sign on air.

It was a huge misunderstanding, but Ed Sullivan decided to cancel Mason's contract on TV, and because of this, he did not appear on TV for 20 years.

In 1962 he released his debut LP, 'I'm the Greatest Comedian in the World, Only Nobody Knows It Yet', followed by 'I Want to Leave You with the Words of a Great Comedian'.

Mason continued to do live stand-up. In 1969 he had a record 97 date run on Broadway (a record which stood for many years). He also appeared in a few films, 'The Jerk' and 'History of the World Part 1.', and several albums were released of his live shows *(which as a young boy of 10, I was introduced to by my dad)*.

Jackie was my inspiration to not only do stand-up but encompass being Jewish and talking about it on stage to a generation of people who have never heard about what it's like being Jewish. I remember one quote (more of his to follow) which inspired me to do my little bit in my act.

'You can't please everyone. I have a girlfriend; I think she's the most wonderful person in the world. That's to me. But to my wife...'

For Jackie Mason, more Broadway followed: The man was prolific in his on-stage stand-up performances:

Between 1986-1987, he had a two-year run of 'The World According to Me'. Its first run was for 367 performances, and its second run 203, for which Jackie won a Tony award. He also did a shot-run sitcom 'Chicken Soup'.

In 1990, 'An audience with Jackie Mason' aired in the UK, and he appeared in another Broadway show.

Between 1994-1955 he had a 347-performance run of the 'Politically Incorrect' show on Broadway.

In 1996 he was back in the UK for 'Jackie Mason at the London Palladium'.

Between 1996-1997, he appeared in two Broadway (one-person shows) shows, 'Love Thy Neighbour' and 'Much Ado About Everything', showing for 225 and 183 performances, respectively.

In 2002 he appeared in 'Prune Danish', followed by 'Freshly Squeezed', between 2005-2006. His runs continued with 'The Ultimate Jew' in 2008 and 'Fearless' in 2012.

Jackie also wrote several books which explained 'How to Talk Jewish'.

Jackie's Famous quotes:

'I have enough money to last me the rest of my life…unless I have to buy something.'

'It's no longer a question of staying healthy. It's a question of finding a sickness you like.'

'80% of married men cheat in America. The rest cheat in Europe.'

'It's easy to tell the difference between Jews and Gentiles. After a show, all the gentiles are saying, 'Have a drink? Want a drink? Let's have a drink!' While all the Jews are saying, 'Have you eaten yet? Want a piece of cake? Let's have some cake!'

'I always thought music was more important than sex…then I thought if I don't hear a concert for a year and a half, it doesn't bother me.'

'I talk to myself because I like dealing with a better class of person.'

'I was so self-conscious; every time football players went into a huddle, I thought they were talking about me.'

'Did you know that the Jews invented Sushi? That's right…2 Jews bought a restaurant with no kitchen.'

Henry Churniavsky's (additional) insight into having a girlfriend

You should never look back with regret. No point dwelling on the past! That's what people say, well, sod you. There are lots of things I would change. I remember one particular event. It involved a girl; this girl, let's call her for this story 'Bitch Jenny'! She is another reason I am neurotic. Well, she ruined the summer of '78. We had been dating for a few months but could not take the relationship to the next level as I lived at home, and my mum was always on duty, and she lived with her strict family. I was offered a villa in Greece for a week in the summer, for free. I decided to ask her to come away, and she was really happy. Gd, I was excited. Sun, sea and hopefully...! All was great in the lead up to the day; we were both excited and could not wait. I met her on the day as her parents dropped her off at the airport. We got through security, got on the plane, put our seat belts on and as we sat in our seats, she turned to me and said, 'I think we should just go as friends.' WTF, WTF friends!

I have friends, friends I could have taken, FFS it was supposed to be me, and my girlfriend and I wanted sex!

It was turning into a nightmare, and it got worse - she took the only bedroom, and I had the sofa. She cooked breakfast...for herself, not me. We were cut-off from any major town. She would just go out the back and sunbathe (topless!!) and not engage in any conversation with me. At night we went to local restaurants, and all she did was read her book. It was the longest seven days of my life. Oh, by the way, when we got home, we split for good.

Henry Churniavsky's insight into Sushi

Sushi: It's not real food...it's not even a meal, at best, a snack. It has a texture of snot. People are snobbish about sushi – it's exotic - it's not! It's international! - It's raw fish. Have you seen those restaurants were sushi is on the conveyor belt? This is salmonella on a rail track! I was once in a sushi bar, and I kid you not, the conveyor belt (of salmonella) was going around and around, and a piece just flipped over! This is not food - it's a pet you eat alive.

1930

Totie Fields 1930 – 1978

Totie Fields (Sophie Feldman) was born in Hartford, Connecticut, the USA, in 1930.

Known as 'The Raucous-Voiced' comedian, this American stand-up comedian found fame in the 1960s and 1970s, especially around Copacabana in New York. Ill health dogged Totie for many years, and she passed away far too early.

Aged 20, she was performing in comedy clubs. She married and moved to New York and confined herself to performing in nightclubs in the area. She managed to get on to the 'Ed Sullivan Show' and other TV shows, which gave her the opportunity to do some Las Vegas shows. TV appearances continued shows like the 'Johnny Carson Show', 'Mike Douglas Show' and 'Merv Griffith Show'. She also appeared on 'Here's Lucy.'

Her comedy was self-deprecating, using her size and weight as the primary source for her act. Her act was mixed with music.

In 1978 she was voted 'Entertainer of the Year' and 'Female Comedy Star of the Year' by the American Guild of Variety Artists. She was an early Joan Rivers who would love to pick on the audience.

Totie's Famous quotes:

'I've been on a diet for two weeks, and all I've lost is two weeks.'

'Shirley Temple had charisma as a child. But it cleared up as an adult.'

'I exercise daily to keep my figure. I keep patting my hand against the bottom of my chin. It works too. I have the thinnest fingers in town.'

After having one leg amputated due to a blood clot, she said, 'I've waited all my life to say this…I weigh less than Elizabeth Taylor.'

'Happiness is getting a brown gravy satin on a brown dress.'

'A diet is a system of starving yourself to death so you can live a little longer.'

'I ran two miles every day for three months and did not lose a lb. The only thing I got was chaffing.'

Henry Churniavsky's (additional) insight into weight issues

I've always had a weight problem; it's not my fault but my mother's. First, can I explain Jewish people do not have weight problems? If male, not a problem; it's

slow metabolism. A female, again if Jewish, not a problem; it's a thyroid issue.
The Jewish idea of a diet is to share a dessert.

During the time that I was writing this book, I was messaged by a gentleman in Southern California, Michael Broido. His wife was called Saralee. They were married on June 26th, 1971 and honeymooned in Lake Tahoe. Around 3 days after the wedding, they went to see The Totie Fields Show. They were seated in the front section of the Casino Theater. Totie started to talk to them from the stage and she could hear their replies. As part of her warm-up, she asked if there were any newlyweds in the audience and of course they raised their hands. 'How long have you been married?' Michael replied, '3 days,' Totie came back 'What? Married 3 days and out of bed already.'

Thank you Michael Broido – this is in honour of your late wife Saralee who passed away aged 72 in 2019 (MHDSRIP).

1931/32

Mike Nichols (1931 – 2014) & Elaine May (1932 -)

Mike Nichols (Mikhail Igor Peschkowsky) was born in Berlin, Germany, in 1931. Nichols arrived in America with his parents at the age of three. He was a film and theatre director, producer, actor and comedian. Nichols' parents were Brigitte and Pavel Peschkowsky. Pavel was a physician who was born in Vienna; his parents were wealthy and lived in Siberia. Nichol's mother's family were German Jews. Mike was distantly related to Albert Einstein.

Nichols became an Academy Award winner for directing 'The Graduate'. He was also a director on Broadway and was part of 'Neil Simon's Barefoot in the Park', 'The Odd Couple' and films such as 'Who's afraid of Virginia Woolf'.

In the early years (1953), Nichols was method acting in New York, but the lack of stage work forced him back to Chicago, where he joined 'The Compass Players'.

Elaine May was also born in Pennsylvania in 1932. An American comedian, screenwriter, director and actress whose screenwriting credentials earned her two Academy Award nominations for 'Heaven Can Wait' (1978) and 'Primary Colors' (1998).

May's father, Jack Berlin, travelled with a Yiddish theatre, and May started her stage career at the age of three. Her mother, Ida, was an actress. The family had to move back to New York when May was 11, as her father had passed away. In 1950 she moved to Chicago, and like Nichols, joined 'The Compass Players'.

The Compass Players were an improv theatre group, which included comedy sketches. Nichols and May hit it off from the start, and after the group finished in 1957, Nichols & May formed a stage act. In 1958 they set themselves up in New York as 'Nichols & May'. Sell-out shows followed, and reviews such as 'Startling', 'New' and 'As Fresh, as Could Be'.

Satirical clichés and character forms were the basis for their act. May showed that as a female, she could succeed in live comedy. Their act was pitched as 'snob and mob appeal' - a different style for the time. Nichols created the structure of their material while May came up with other ideas in creating 'scenes'.

The duo influenced the new generation, including Lily Tomlin and Steve Martin. Their act over the next four years was 'One of the comic meteors in the sky.' (Dick Cavett)

In 1960 a Broadway debut, 'An Evening with Mike Nichols and Elaine May' saw them win a Grammy.

At the end of four years at the height of their success, they called it a day. As Nichols & May, they had created a new 'Age of Irony' for comedy. This was picked up by artists such as Steve Martin, Bill Murray and David Letterman.

As you can see, they left at the top of their game, and they both went onto have successful solo careers in show business.

Nichols' & May's Famous Quotes:

May: 'You know how sometimes you lie in bed at night and think, 'What if the law of gravity just wears out and let's go and I drift into space?' Does that ever make you anxious?'

'The only safe thing is to take a chance.'

Nichols: 'The whole point about laughter is it's like mercury: you can't catch it; you can't catch what motivates it - that's why it's funny.'

Nichols & May did a routine around a phone conversation between a mother and a son; she is complaining he never rings her. Here is part of the sketch:
Son: (Nichols) 'How are you? Are you ok? What's the matter?'
Mother: (May) 'I'm sick...it's nothing.'
Son: 'I'm sorry.'

Mother: 'It's nothing...you know what it is? It's my nerves. I went to the doctors; the doctor said, 'You're a very nervous, very highly-strung woman...'

Son (interrupting but not heard): 'Gd knows you're right, that's true.'

Mother: 'You know I cannot stand the slightest aggravation. I said to the doctor, I know, I know, but you see, doctor, I have this son, and he is so busy, too busy to pick up the phone to his mother. I told him, I told the doctor, and do you know what, that man turned pale. He said, I have been a doctor for 35 years, and I have never heard of a son too busy to call his mother. And Arthur, that man is a doctor.'

Son: 'Mother, please, what are they going to do?'

Mother: 'I'm going to be away for a while; they are going to x-ray my nerves, look; it's nothing forget it. Someday, Arthur, you'll get married and have children of your own, and honey, when you do, I can only pray that they make you suffer like you made me. That's all I pray for Arthur. That's a mother's prayer.'

Son: 'Ok, Mum, thanks for calling.'

Mother: 'You're very sarcastic! I'm sorry, I'm sorry I bothered you. But I hope I didn't make you feel bad?'

Son: 'Are you kidding? I feel awful.'

Mother: 'Oh, honey, if I could only believe that I'd be the happiest mother in the world.'

'Jewish introspection and Jewish humour are a way of surviving; if you're not handsome and you're not athletic, and you're not rich, there's still one last hope with girls, which is being funny.'

Henry Churniavsky's (additional) insight into being Jewish and girls

Being a young Jewish person is a nightmare. From a young age, my friends and I would travel to Manchester in search of the perfect woman. I know we were young, and thought a Manchester girl would be perfect. Sorry Manchester, it wasn't to be.

The issue was Jewish girls are different from Gentile girls, and I mean that in a nice way. You would go to a dance; yes, that's what we called them when we were young! Get over it! The issue was you could get talking to a girl when suddenly this would come out; 'What's the family name? What are your grandparents called on both sides? What area do you live in, in Liverpool? What is the family's original name? What do your parents do for a living? Is there a family business? What do you do? (When do these girls take a breath!) ...For Gd's sake, I'm only 13. I only have a paper round; give me a break! This line of questioning went on for years; at every function we would go to even into our 20s.

I was never great at chatting up women, and I remember one night I was having a drink with friends at a bar, and I was egged on to go and ask this girl out who I had been looking at for ages. I took up the courage and went over and said, 'Would you mind if I chatted with you for a while and buy you a drink?' She looked at me and YELLED at the top of her voice, 'No, I won't come over to your place tonight!' Everyone just stopped what they were doing and looked at me, walking back to my friends, who were pissing themselves as they thought it was so funny. A few minutes later, the girl came over to me to apologise. 'I'm sorry if I embarrassed you, I am a postgraduate student in psychology, and I am studying human reactions to embarrassing situations.' I turned to her and YELLED, 'What do you mean? You will come home with me for two hundred pounds.' You can see why I was single for so long!!!

Oh, there is more, I can assure you. Maybe later!

1933

Joan Rivers 1933 – 2014

Joan Rivers (Joan Alexandra Molinsky) was born in Brooklyn, New York, in 1933. She was a great American comedian, actress, writer, producer, TV host and entrepreneur. Joan was 'controversial', very self-deprecating and sharply attacked celebrities and politicians. She had what we Jewish people would say was 'Chutzpah.' Rivers was the first real female stand-up comic. Her catchphrases of 'Don't start', 'Oh grow up', 'Oh please' and 'Can we talk' were part of her act. Nothing was off-limits to Rivers, especially during her stand-up. She was one of the first 'unfiltered' comics.

Joan River's parents were Russian immigrants, Beatrice and Meyer C Molinsky. She showed an interest in theatre at an early age but still wanted to graduate, and she ended up getting a B.A. in English Literature and Anthropology. Before she got the show business bug, she did several jobs, and she also changed her name on advisement from her agent, Tony Rivers.

In the late 1950s, Rivers was in an Off-Broadway play, Driftwood, with Barbara Streisand and was performing in many comedy clubs in Greenwich Village, New York City *(in 2018, I was lucky to gig in Greenwich Village, which was a highlight for me in my stand up)*. During this era, she was gigging with Woody Allen and George Carlin.

Gigs at the Catskills followed, but it was not until 1961 she had her breakthrough performance at the Second City in Chicago. She was dubbed 'The best girl since Elaine May'.

During 1963-1964 Rivers teamed up with Jim Connell and Jake Holmes as a cabaret act 'Jim, Jake & Joan'. They also made a film, but the trio split shortly after.

In 1965 Rivers made her first appearance on the 'Johnny Carson Show'. She started on the show as a joke writer. It was the breakthrough she needed and was the start of a friendship with Carson, which lasted for years. Joan eventually went on to do over 80 shows and even stood in for Carson when he went on holiday.

It was from there she started making more guest appearances on several shows: Ed Sullivan, Mike Douglas and Dick Calvert's. In the 1960s, Rivers also released two comedy albums.

Rivers married for a second time in 1965 to Edgar Rosenberg. She later quipped, 'I said to my husband Edgar, women are like wine, the older we get, the mellower we become. So, he locked me in the cellar.'

The 1970s saw her success continue, with guest spots on the circuit and appearances on TV shows, including a guest spot on 'Here's Lucy'; she also appeared in Las Vegas. From the early and mid-1980s, Rivers became more successful in stand-up and on TV. In 1983 she performed at Carnegie Hall and followed it with 'An Audience with Joan Rivers'. A best-selling comedy album followed, for which she received a Grammy.

By 1983 she was a permanent host on 'The Tonight Show'. In 1984 Rivers made her debut in 'An Audience with…' on British TV and repeated it with a new show in 2006. In 1986 Johnny Carson signed a new two-year contract, but Rivers was not offered anything new. She felt that, at the time, she was not in NBC's long-term plans. At the same time, FOX approached her with a rival show, and this (of course) affected her relationship with her good friend Carson (in fact, Carson banned her from appearing on the show, and his successors continued the ban until 2014).

However, the FOX show did not last. Fox wanted to fire the show producer, Rivers husband Edgar, and eventually, they fired both of them. This was a very low point in her life. Her husband committed suicide three months later. Her career also stalled, but in late 1989 a new daytime show, 'The Joan Rivers Show', brought her back to the limelight.

The 1990s saw Rivers win an Emmy for her daytime television talk show. She also appeared in a TV film. Rivers began designing jewellery, clothing and beauty products, and QVC sold her collections. The mid-1990s saw Rivers hosting pre-awards shows.

Rivers also co-wrote a play about Sally Marr, a stand-up comic who was more famous for being Lenny Bruce's mother. This went on to do 50 performances on Broadway, and she received nominations for a Drama Desk Award and a Tony Award.

Radio also was another outlet for her in New York.

The 2000s saw Rivers continue her career guest-starring on various TV shows, and in 2007 she performed at the Liverpool Empire Theatre at the 79th Royal Variety Show.

She wrote books and continued with her work in TV and film until she died in 2014.

Joan's Famous quotes:

'The worst thing anyone has ever said to me is that I'm 50. Which I am. Oh, that bitch. I was hurt.'

'When a man has a birthday, he takes a day off. When a woman has a birthday, she takes at least three years off.'

'I don't exercise. If Gd wanted us to bend over, he'd have put diamonds on the floor.'

'My routines come out of total unhappiness. My audiences are my group therapy.'

'The average aeroplane is 16 years old, and so is the average aeroplane meal.'

'Before we make love, my husband takes a painkiller.'

'Is Elizabeth Taylor fat? Her favourite food is seconds.'

'It's been so long since I've had sex; I've forgotten who ties up whom.'

'This woman was so fat that one day she was wearing a red dress, and 30 children tried to board her.'

'I said to my husband; my looks have gone, my stomach has gone, say something nice about my legs. He said blue goes with everything.'

'The first time I see a jogger smiling. I'll consider it.'

Joan talked a lot about sex. So, I have added a few old Jewish jokes on the subject.

Did you hear about the guy who called his girlfriend 'Mezuzah' because she liked to be kissed?
Victor and Leah were an elderly couple who had been dating for some time. They decided to get married, but first, they needed to discuss how their marriage might work. They discussed finances, living arrangements, health and lastly, sex. 'How do you feel about sex, Leah?' Victor asked.

'Oh, I like to have it infrequently,' she replied. 'Oh, was that one word or two?'

A Hassidic Jew was in a lift with a beautiful woman, who, in fact, was a prostitute. She turned to him and said, 'Are you a Hassidic Jew?'
'Yes.' He replied.
'OMG.' She said, 'It's always been a wish of mine, as a high-class hooker, to make mad passionate love to a Hassidic Jew.'
He just looked at her and said, 'Ah-ha.'
She continued, 'Look, I want to take you to my penthouse flat at the top here, slowly undress you, cover you with cream and ride you all night.'
He replied, 'Ah-ha.'
She went on, 'Then I want us to sleep the night away with you in my arms and in the morning make you a magnificent breakfast and do it all over again, is that ok?'
The man looked at her and said, 'Well, I can see what's in it for you, but what's in it for me?'

Henry Churniavsky's more insight into keeping fit

Have you got a Fitbit or Apple watch? Ok, they have some good features, don't get me wrong. It tells you the time. It also has some other apps which I am not sure about:

Disturbed sleep - Do I need to know if I have had a disturbed night's sleep? I will know if I have had a bad sleep; I will be knackered all day!

Pulse rate - Yes, very useful. If I am breathing, my pulse is ok. Once I flat-lined, I thought I was dead; then I realised my battery was dead.

Text messages - Yes, ok, I'll get a text, but it's so small I need a magnifying glass to read it.

Calorie counter - Do I need a watch to tell me that I am a fat f**k! What I need is an electric shock when I open the fridge.

Oxygen rate - Do I need this? I know when I am out of oxygen…it's called wheezing!

I read something recently that told me I could get an app on my phone, which lets me know when my joint bank account goes overdrawn by giving me a short electric shock. If my wife is shopping, it will look like I'm having an epileptic fit.

My Apple watch is 'doing my head in!' I was at home, watching TV. And not long after I had sat down when it bleeped, 'Achievement' – sarcastic t**t! Just cos I stood up to go to the toilet.

1934

Marty Feldman 1934 – 1982

Marty (Martin Alan) Feldman was born in 1934 in London's East End. He may not be a typical 'stand-up' comic, but he did start his career as a stand-up before becoming one of the most famous faces of British comedy. He was a British actor, comedian and comedy writer and deserves a mention. Marty was known for his prominent eyes and wit.

Feldman was the son of Cecilia and Myer Feldman. They were Jewish immigrants from Kiev, Ukraine. Myer was a gown manufacturer.

At an early age, Marty suffered from thyroid disease and developed Graves' Ophthalmology which caused his eyes to protrude. He also suffered due to a car crash, a boating accident and reconstructive surgery, so he did not have an easy start in life. Eventually, Myer and his family moved to North London, but it caused issues at school for Marty, and he was bullied. He had also been expelled 12 times by the time he left school at 15. Leaving school, he went to Margate in the summer to work and became part of a trio 'Morris, Marty & Mitch'. Over the next few years, the trio toured variety clubs and US Army bases performing music, slapstick and dance routines. But they were not a runaway success.

In the early 50s, during the final years of variety, Feldman saw acts like Jimmy James, Max Miller and Freddie Frinton perform comedy, and it inspired him to move back home and become a writer.

He started with Radio shows, 'Take It From Here', where he met Barry Took. More radio followed with 'Educating Archie'. Then came television; 'Sgt. Major Snudge' and 'Private Bisley' (39 episodes), 'The Army Game' and also radio, 'Round the Horne'.

Feldman was also instrumental in writing catchphrases for the stars of the day: 'Ullo, it's me Twinkletoes', for Bernard Bresslaw; 'Hello, Honky-Tonk', for Dick Emery. As well as penning famous sketches such as the famous 'class sketch' for 'The Frost Report'.

In 1966 Feldman became the main writer for BBC's 'The Frost Report' with many notable comedians. Marty even performed in 'At Last the 1948 Show', where he was one of the writers and performers for the 'Four Yorkshiremen' sketch. This led to Feldman's own show, and movies in America followed.

Gene Wilder and Mel Brooks offered Feldman a part in 'Young Frankenstein', which was a universal hit. Feldman played Igor (pronounced Eye-gore, as a response to Wilder's pronunciation of his character Fronk -en -Schteen); it was in this film Marty had the line, 'Hump, what hump?'

Feldman's career took off again with parts in 'Sherlock Holmes Smarter Brother' and 'Silent Movie', a perfect film for Feldman's natural slapstick. It was from here that Feldman was offered £5 million to make his own feature film, 'The Last Remake of Beau Geste' in 1977. Feldman also wrote and directed the film, 'In Gd we Trust', a film with Andy Kaufman and Richard Prior.

He died in 1982 in Mexico City from a heart attack. Only 48. He is buried next to his idol, Buster Keaton.

Marty's Famous quotes:

'Comedy, like sodomy, is an unnatural act.'

'In retrospect, come to think of it, isn't everything seen in retrospect?'

'Money can't buy you poverty.'

'Doubts are about the only certainties I have right now, yes.'

'Humour evolves as you evolve as a person; you do it for the same reason you paint a moustache on the Mona Lisa. It's a spontaneous demonstration of anarchy.'

'I loved the idea of seeing myself in print, though I immediately felt vulnerable because my stuff was now open to criticism.'

'The pen is mightier than the sword and considerably easier to write with.'

'My grandfather used to work for your grandfather. Of course, the rates have gone up.'

'I think the success went straight to my crutch.'

'I won the award for being the best loser.'

'I'm too old to die young, too old to grow up.'

Henry Churniavsky's insight into his getting old, having your prostate checked

I recently had to have my prostate checked. There are two ways. One is a periscope down your willy... "No effin way that's happening today!" The second, and I am sorry, guys, is a finger up the butt. Again, I'm not enamoured with this either, I can tell you.
Anyway, the date is in the diary, and I go. Tears are welling up; I am lying on the slab in my gown (open at the back) with my knees up to my chest.
In walks the consultant; I feel his presence behind me. I hear a rubber glove being put on. I now hear the sound of lubrication...it's time. A tear drops to my cheek (face,

by the way) as the Dr says, "Relax, Henry, Relax." How can you relax with a finger up the butt hole!!! He continues, "Relax, Henry and don't worry about the erection."

I answer very quickly, "I haven't got an erection Dr?"

"Who said it was you?" was the reply. I gulped and tried to relax until I noticed that both his hands were on my shoulders!!!

He then inserted, without asking, two fingers! I screamed "WTF are you doing now?"

His reply, "I'm going for a second opinion."

Eventually, the experience stopped. He withdrew his finger, took his gloves off and, without a word, started to leave the room. As he left, the nurse entered and came up to me and uttered those five words which will haunt me forever... "Who the f**k was that?"

1935

Woody Allen 1935 -

Woody Allen (Allan Stewart Konigsberg) was born in Brooklyn, New York, in 1935. He is an American actor, director, writer & comedian.
Before Allen emerged as one of the foremost American filmmakers of the 20th century, he was a stand-up comic.

Woody's mother was Nettie, a bookkeeper at the family's delicatessen. Her husband, Martin Konigsberg, was a jewellery engraver and waiter. Allen's parents were raised in Manhattan, and his grandparents came from Austria and Lithuania. They spoke German, Hebrew and Yiddish.

Allen started writing short jokes at the age of 15, and he sent them to various Broadway writers.
At 17, he changed his name and, in 1953, enrolled in New York's University film program.
Allen sent some of his jokes to an agent, David O. Alber, who sold them to newspaper journalists; he paid Allen $20 a week.

At 19, he was asked to join NBC's development programme, and he started to write for the 'Ed Sullivan Show', Sid Caesar and 'The Tonight Show'. He also worked alongside Mel Brooks, Carl Reiner, Neil Simon and many others. He also penned material for Pat Boone.

Allen also worked on the Buddy Hackett sitcom and other shows.

He would often sit for up to 15 hours at a time so that he could improve his writing.

In 1960, Allen took on a new manager, Jack Rollins, who was also managing Nichols & May. Allen's stand-up era was between 1960 and 1969. Rollins advised Allen to do more jokes at the clubs, but he resisted for a while. One night he watched Mort Sahl at a gig, and this pushed Allen to perform his first professional debut at the Blue Angel in 1960; he was introduced by a well-known comedian at the time, Shelly Berman.

Allen's jokes came from his own life experiences, and his deadpan, serious outlook and demeanour were new on the scene. One thing that stood out was Allen made the material seem as if it was ad-libbed, but he rehearsed all his lines and very rarely improvised.

By 1963 he was on the 'Johnny Carson Show', and he was a regular on the show for about nine years. He even hosted the show several times.

Allen even found time to release three albums of live material in 1964 and 1968. These have been reissued over the years (in 1972 – two LP's 'The Night Club Years 64-68', and another, later, titled 'Stand-up Comic'. In

2014 all three were reissued along with some unreleased work.

Towards the end of the 1960s, Allen looked for a new challenge and became a playwright; he produced plays such as "Play it Again Sam' on Broadway in 1969, which had 453 performances.

In 1981 'The Floating Light Bulb', also, on Broadway ran for 65 performances and in 2011, a one-act play 'Honeymoon Motel' opened on Broadway, and in 2014 the musical 'Bullets Over Broadway'.

Besides this, Allen had an amazing film career with films such as 'What's New, Pussycat' (1965), 'Bananas' (1971), 'Everything You Always Wanted To Know About Sex' (1972), 'Sleeper' (1973), 'Annie Hall' (1977) and 'Manhattan' (1979) which also won four Academy Awards.

In the 1980s and 1990s, Allen showed no let-up in his filmography, which included 'Hannah and Her Sisters' (1986), 'Crimes and Misdemeanours' (1989), and in 2013 'Blue Jasmine' won Allen another Academy Award.

Allen had a long-time interest in playing jazz and was subject to a documentary in 1998 – 'Wild Man Blues'. He plays every Monday in Manhattan at the Carnegie Hotel.

In 2001 Allen announced on Jay Leno chat show that he had finally stopped seeing his psychoanalyst, to which

Leno said, 'If, after 40 years, you've married your own daughter, then I guess you can figure it isn't working' …Ouch!!

Woody's Famous quotes:

'The best thing to do is to behave in a manner befitting one's age. If you are 16 or under, try not to go bald.'

'I will not eat oysters. I want my food dead. Not sick, not wounded, dead.'

'I don't want to achieve immortality through my work. I want to achieve it through not dying.'

'My parents stayed together for 40 years, but it was out of spite.'

'Basically, my wife was immature. I'd be at home in the bath, and she'd come in and sink my boats.'

'My love life is terrible. The last time I was inside a woman was when I visited the Statue of Liberty.'

'It's not that I'm afraid to die. I just don't want to be there when it happens.'

'If only Gd gave me a clear sign: like making a large deposit in my name at a Swiss bank.'

'The prison psychiatrist asked me if I thought sex was dirty. I told him only when it's done right.'

'Two elderly women are in a restaurant, and one of them says, 'Boy, the food in this place is really terrible!'
The other one says, 'Yeah, I know and such small portions.'

Well, that's essentially how I feel about life. Full of loneliness and misery and suffering - and it's all over too soon.'

'Sex without love is a meaningless experience, but as far as meaningless experiences go, it's pretty damn good.'

'I don't think my parents liked me. They put a live teddy bear in my crib.'

'In my house, I'm the boss - My wife is just the decision-maker.'

Woody talked a lot about his wife. So, I have added a few old Jewish jokes on the subject:

Moshe goes up to a beautiful woman in the supermarket and says to her, 'I've lost my wife in here, and I would be very happy if you could find some time to talk to me for a few minutes.'
She asks, 'Why on earth do you want me to do that?'

Moshe replies, 'Because every time I talk to a beautiful woman, my wife always appears out of nowhere.'

Two rabbis were discussing the decline in morals in today's society.
'I didn't sleep with my wife before I was married,' said the first. 'Did you?'
'I don't know, what was her maiden name?' the other rabbi said.

An old Jewish proverb: 'A Jewish wife will forgive and forget, but she'll never forget what she forgave.'

Henry Churniavsky's insight into parents

Everyone grows up, and we have our own issues, but for us Jewish boys, we get our issues very young, and I mean very young. There are a number of these issues which affect us:
Firstly, my dad decided to find a new use for his cigar cutter – yes, at eight days old, I was circumcised with a cigar cutter. I wouldn't mind, but my dad never smoked cigars.

1936

David Brenner 1936 – 2014

David Brenner was born in Philadelphia in 1936; Brenner was an American stand-up comedian, actor and author. He was one of the most frequent guests on 'The Tonight Show' with Johnny Carson in the 1970s and 1980s.

Brenner is considered to be the pioneer of observational comedy.

David's father, Louis, was the vaudeville comedian, singer and dancer, Louis Murphy. He had to give up his career in entertainment to please David's grandfather, Louis' dad, as he was a local rabbi, and it caused a lot of issues, especially working on the Sabbath.

Brenner, before comedy took hold, was a writer, director and producer. He had done 115 TV documentaries and won over 30 awards, including an Emmy.

In 1969 he did his first improv paid gig in New York, and more gigs followed in the famous Greenwich Village.

In 1976, he was cast in a comedy TV series, which was cancelled as it was considered the 'wrong time', as Brenner portrayed one of the first gay characters in an American sitcom.

In 1983, he released a comedy album which came out along with five books. Richard Lewis called him 'The King of Hip, observational comedy.'

In 1986, Brenner hosted a late-night talk show for one season.

In 2009, he released another comedy album.

Brenner's observational comedy inspired Jerry Seinfeld and Paul Reiser. Brenner came up with his act from everyday life, social and political issues.

In 1995, he appeared at the 'Just for Laughs Festival' in Montreal.

Brenner died in March 2014, but as late as December 2013, Brenner was still doing stand-up and did a four-day gig.

David's Famous quotes:

'A vegetarian is a person who won't eat anything that can have children.'

'I don't like to watch golf on TV because I can't stand people who whisper.'

'I want my tombstone to read: If this is a joke, I don't get it.'

'Nothing is going to stop Mike Tyson that doesn't have a motor attached.'

'When I go to a bar, I don't go looking for a girl who knows the capital of Maine.'

Henry Churniavsky's insight into going into a bar/club

Dating in Liverpool had its own issues, especially as we had turned 17 and wanted to go into the City Centre. I remember in the late 1970s going with my mate into the city centre and clubbing on a Saturday night.

We arrived in the back streets of Liverpool at this slightly run-down club, and we knocked on the door. A bouncer came out and asked, 'Yes, what do you want?'

'We would like to come into your club, please.' Was our reply.

'Are any of yous carryin a knife or anyting like that?'

'No, we are not,' I said, 'We are respectable people, I can assure you.'

'Alright.' The bouncer replied and gave us two knives, 'Keep des with you and drop them back at reception when you leave.'

We should have known by that what sort of place it was going to be, but we paid our entrance fee. Question - why is it good looking girls always get in free, and boys have to pay? They usually end up paying for the girl's drinks as well.

It should also have been a warning as we entered; the music playing was the Bee Gees, 'Staying Alive, Staying Alive'; not a great omen.

Anyway, we were in a proper night club, and there were women, loads of them. I was looking around, and *this girl rolled her eye at me (I picked it up and rolled it back...thank you, Mr Tommy Cooper). I noticed this girl looking at me, so I went over and asked her for a dance, she said yes...well in!! After a few dances, she turned to me and, in the broadest Scouse accent, said, 'Will you dance with me mate; I've gotta go for a shite.' NOW, most men (boys in this case) would stop and re-evaluate what had happened, but let's be honest, I am no Brad Pitt, and to be fair, this girl had three things going for her. 1. She was female. 2. She was female and breathing. 3. She was female, breathing and still talking to me. Oh, and 4. She had amazing knockers (sorry, it was the hormones).*

I decided after the last dance to ask her out on a proper date. So, I took her to a pub around the corner from my house, and after that, I invited her back to my family home. I did stress we had to be really quiet as I did not want to wake up my parents.

We sat on the couch and started kissing (I think it was called snogging the face off her). My hormones were all over the place, and I probably got a bit carried away as I went straight for the crotch! BIG, BIG mistake, she bolted upright and smacked me right across the face and said, 'Hey lad, tits first I'm not a slag.' So, now you know how I met my wife - only kidding (she might read this one day!).

Arnold Brown 1936 –

Arnold Brown, born in Glasgow in 1936, is a Scottish, Jewish Comedian. He was a key figure in the 'alternative' comedy scene in the early 1980s. An accountant by trade *(no stereotyping here, by the way!)*, Brown's slow meandering style looked at observational comedy, which won him a Perrier Award in Edinburgh in 1987. He is regarded as a comic philosopher and was once described as 'the missing link between generations of comics', he has the catchphrases and eccentricities of his seniors, and the references and political barbs of the younger generation.'

Brown came to prominence in the early 1980s working with Alexei Sayle and Rik Mayall at the Comedy Store and The Comic Strip.

Brown won the first prestigious Perrier Award at the Edinburgh Festival in 1987. He is probably the only Glaswegian, Jewish ex-chartered accountant stand-up around. *(I think I'm unique; Scouse, Jewish drug dealer - not many of them around!)*

Brown was part of 'The Comic Strip' (who made films) in 1981, and later, he appeared on television. His stage show 'Comfort and Joy' was a great success.

He had TV appearances on 'The Brown Show' and 'The Young Ones'. He also received a Scottish Comedy Lifetime Achievement Award in 2014.

In 1989-90 Arthur Brown and Company were on Radio Four. He also produced the BBC Two sitcom 'The Brown Man' in 1990.

Brown played in London's Dominion Theatre and in a major international comedy festival in Edinburgh and Montreal.

In 1994 his first book was released, 'Are You Looking at Me, Jimmy'.

In 2000 he appeared in 'Talking Pictures', ' Live from London', 'Word of Mouth' and in a play called 'Sense of Balance'.

Brown has also appeared in the feature films- 'Personal Services', 'Comfort and Joy', 'Esther Khan', 'Liam' and in 2002 'Young Adam'.

Brown released CD, a 'Guide to the Perplexed' and a video – 'Live at Hackney Empire'. Also, a DVD –'Jokes I Have Known'.

He has also written and performed in 'Are You Feeling Funny?', which looks at the effects of laughter on health.

Arnold's Famous quotes:

'I enjoy using the comedy technique of self-deprecation - but I'm not very good at it.'

'The secret to comedy is... timing. For example you the audience have come here tonight and if I arrive one week later...that's bad timing. I am a hardened professional, and I notice it makes a difference even one day out.'

'My father was a late developer, and I had the pleasure of watching him grow up. It was embarrassing as I learnt to walk before he did.'

1937

Freddie Roman 1937 -

Freddie Roman (Fred Kirschenbaum) was born in 1937 and grew up in New York. He is an American stand-up comedian who is best known for his gigs at the 'Borscht Belt'.

His father was a shoe salesman, and some of his extended family owned the Crystal Spring Hotel in the Catskills. At 15, Roman was given a chance to MC; he became a teenage comedian, but he left to help his father out in his shoe business, as he married after he left school and needed to make a living. He eventually went on to own a shoe store but realised that comedy was for him. He sold the store after six years and started selling life insurance, which freed up time to do comedy.

At his height, he headlined at many venues, including Caesars Palace in Las Vegas and Harrah's in Atlantic City.

He was a member of the famous 'Friars Club', and they liked him so much they changed their rules so he could stay on as Dean.

He co-wrote and starred in the Broadway hit 'Catskills on Broadway', with Dick Capri, Mal Z. Lawrence and Louise DuArt in 2003. Roman was also in the 2010 show 'Sunrise Lakes Phase IV'.

Between 1987 and 2006, he performed in several films and has made numerous television appearances, including 'Funny Already' - a history of Jewish comedy, 'The Tonight Show Starring Johnny Carson', 'Friars Club' roasts and many more.

Freddie's Famous quotes:

'You come home with 100 rolls of toilet paper; you pray for diarrhoea.'

'11 years ago, I became President (Friars Club) for two years. I'm like the Fidel Castro of comedians. I'm President for life.'

'Mike Tyson is an interesting story. He's the only person in America who's driving a $250,000 car, who actually made the license plates for that car.'

'A man goes to see the doctor. He says, 'Doctor, I have a problem. I can't pee anymore.'
The doctor looks at him and says, 'How old are you?'
'Ninety -four.'
The doctor says, 'You've peed enough.'

Henry Churniavsky's insight into peeing too much.

It was only recently I found out that there are, in fact, two ways to check your prostate. The first is well known;

it's the finger up the butt, a technique I did not enjoy, to be honest. So a recent visit to the urologist for an issue I won't go into detail on; it was suggested I needed a cystoscopy. "A what?" was my response. I am advised by the consultant that it entails, and men cross your legs now, a camera going down your penis. "Oh, really," I exclaimed. "And will I be out for this procedure?" I am advised that knocking me out is not going to happen, but I am informed my penis will be numbed, oh really. "How?"

"Oh, just a small prick," the female consultant says, and I sense a wry smile!

So, I am booked in for the following week, when this female consultant will grab my cock and ram a Nikon camera with a zoom lens into it. The day arrives, and I am lying on the slab in a gown with an audience of four people as the Consultant advises me to relax. Yeah, that's going to happen. She grabs my penis, numbs it and says, "I'm going to flush some water down before we put the camera in."

A bit of water? It's like Niagara Falls getting flushed down your willie, and all you want to do is have a piss.

"Please can you wiggle your toes?" is the next thing I hear - really, I have a fountain of water being flushed, and you want me to do party tricks? Next, I hear, "Pass the camera," and without a word, this steel metal rod is pushed into my willie. WTF is going on, "Just relax, Mr Churney; we are in now." Oh, really, I feel like screaming, take the bloody thing out.

Next, I see a large TV screen with this Nikon camera inside my prostate. If I get a photo of this, it is going on Facebook as THE ultimate selfie.

"Oh, look, everyone, this is what we are looking for." She tells the crowd to gather around my cock and look at the TV screen. The nurse holding my hand is trying to comfort me with words of wisdom. "Soon be over, just relax," then, without a word, I feel the metal rod being removed. Now I am either going to piss myself or have a crap, maybe both.

The consultant says the investigation is inconclusive, and I may have to have an orchidoscopy. I tell her straight, "There is no way you're putting orchids in me; get a vase, like everyone else."

1942

Robert Klein 1942 -

Robert Klein was born in The Bronx, America, in 1942. He was an American stand-up comedian, singer and actor. In the 1970s, he produced a number of comedy albums and was nominated for a Tony award in 1979 for 'They're Playing Our Song'.

Klein was the son of Freida and Benjamin Klein; he was the grandson of Hungarian Jews who arrived in America in the early 20th century.

Klein studied at Yale Drama School, and while he attended there, he wrote a piece of improv which got him hired by Second City. In 1965 he was cast by Mike Nichols in a Broadway musical.

During the 1970s, Klein made a number of TV appearances, including 'The Ed Sullivan Show', and he also produced comedy albums. His 'Watergate Scandal' routine made him, at the time, very popular. In 1986 he began a two-year run with a late-night TV show.

Klein's unique stand-up persona was a hip, but simple man caught up in a modern world, and it made Klein one of the top comics of the last 20 years.

He made many albums – 'The Child of the 1950s', (1973), 'Mind over Matter' (1974), 'New Teeth' (1975). In 1984 HBO did a special – 'The Child of the 1950s', then in 1986 'Robert Klein on Broadway'.

Klein also appeared in movies, which included 'The Owl and the Pussycat', 'Hooper' and 'Primary Colors'.

He also hosted Saturday Night Live - twice. In 2007 HBO produced a DVD compilation from eight shows. He was also considered to be an influence on Jay Leno, as Leno was very influenced by 'The Child of the 1950s'.

Robert's Famous quotes:

'And the only studies were…Rodney Dangerfield was my mentor, and he was my Yale school for comedy.'

'My son has been a class clown, and it sort of ran in the family.'

'In the 1950s, I had a dream about touching a naked woman, and she would turn bronze or a dream about hot dogs chasing donuts through Lincoln tunnel.'

'I have what we call a 'Symphony Act' I'm the only comedian, I think, in the country that does it.'

'Comedy is still alive, and there are still funny people. Jews are still over-represented in comedy and psychiatry and underrepresented in the priesthood. That immigrant Jewish humour is still with us.'

Henry Churniavsky's insight into a bit of Jewish humour

The 'so-called' deadly sins. To a Jewish mother, there is no such thing as the deadly sins, let me explain:

PRIDE: Not a deadly sin if it's one of your offspring. 'My son is a Director of implementing ideas.' This was a Jewish mother about her son. The fact was that he works for his father and does what he is told.

LUST: Jewish men are not great lovers. I remember once being really happy that one night I made love to my wife for an hour and ten minutes. When I informed the wife, she looked at the clock and said, 'Idiot, the clocks have gone forward an hour.'

ENVY: The cornerstone of a Jewish Woman's life. So, envy does not exist as a sin if it's against other women, especially her close friends. Do you remember the famous Jewish joke …?

A man and a woman get on a plane. She is wearing the biggest wedding ring ever. The lady next to her comments. 'I love your diamond; it's so big and beautiful.'

'Oh, this.' Says the woman. 'It's the Plutnick Diamond.'

'Oh really, what is that?' the lady enquires.

'The Plutnick Diamond is famous. It's between the Great Star Diamond and The Star of Africa. But it comes with a curse.'

'A curse, how romantic!' She replied.

'You don't know the curse.'
'What is the curse? Please tell me?'
The woman with the ring looks at the lady and says, 'Mr. Plutnick.'

ANGER: Not if directed by a Jewish woman to her husband. I remember my mother saying my dad only had two faults, everything he said and everything he did.

SLOTH: in Jewish terms, sloth can mean a 'Shmuck.'

Sadie tells Morrie, 'You're a SHMUCK! You always were a SHMUCK, and you always will be a SHMUCK! You look, act and dress like a SHMUCK! You'll be a SHMUCK until the day you die. And if they ever ran a world-wide competition for SHMUCKS, you would be the world's second-biggest SHMUCK!'
'Why only second place?' he asks.
'Because you're a SHMUCK!' she screams.

GLUTTONY: Never, if a mother, or grandmother, has spent time cooking for the family. What would be a sin, BULIMIA? Can you imagine your grandmother discussing that topic? 'Vat is the matter vid you young girl? Is my cooking that bad? Do you know I have slaved in the kitchen for not two or three hours but over five hours, the time is not important, it's made with love! All I have done is make you a snack. All you have had is chicken soup with matzah balls, chopped liver with egg & onion and chala, *and fresh salt beef with latkas. I'm upset with you as you would not have seconds, vat is wrong with you?'*

GREED: It's not greed that is a sin - maybe it gets a bit mixed up with being practical...

1943

Freddie Starr 1943 – 2019

Frederick Leslie Starr was born in Huyton, Liverpool, in 1943. His mother was Jewish and encouraged him at the age of 12 to perform in clubs and pubs *(Probably not the most orthodox Jewish upbringing!).* He became one of the finest English stand-up impressionists. He was also an accomplished singer and actor.

Starr had a colourful upbringing, which goes in a small way to explain his sometimes bizarre behaviour. Aged six, he lost the power of speech for two years and was sent away from home for treatment.

Starr's mother encouraged him, and at the age of 12, pushed him to become a member of the 'Hilda Fallon Roadshow', which he was for five years.

In the early 1960s, Starr was the lead singer of a Merseybeat pop group 'The Midniters' managed by the Beatles manager by Brien Epstein.

In 1967, Freddie Starr appeared on 'Opportunity Knocks', which opened the door for a celebrity lifestyle.

In 1970, he was on the 'Royal Variety Performance' show imitating Mick Jagger to Adolf Hitler.

He had two TV specials, 'An Audience With...' in 1996 and 1997. He also had two TV shows 1993-1994 – 'Freddie Starr' and 1996-1997 – 'The Freddie Starr Show.'

In making great headlines, Starr became a legend - 'Freddie Starr Ate My Hamster'. In 1986, this was the headline in a British newspaper (The Sun); it was a publicity stunt that some of the British readers wanted to believe.

I remember seeing Freddie Starr in concert in his, and my, hometown of Liverpool, and he blew me away with his set. I also met him in Marbella, in Puerto Banus, with my friends one summer, and he was a true gentleman.

Freddie's Famous quote:

'I'm so unlucky that if I was to fall into a barrel of nipples, I'd come out sucking my thumb.'

1944

Harold Ramis 1944 – 2014

Harold Allen Ramis was born in Chicago in 1944. The son of Jewish parents Ruth and Nathan Ramis, owners of ACE Food & Liquor Mart in Chicago. He was an American actor, comedian and writer. He is probably best known for his role in the film 'Ghostbusters' released in 1984.

He also directed many films, including 'Caddyshack' (1980), 'National Lampoon's Vacation' (1983) and Groundhog Day (1993), which he directed and produced. He also directed and produced 'Bedazzled' (2000).

Ramis started writing plays while still at college; he said, 'In my heart, I felt I was a combination of Groucho and Harpo Marx, of Groucho using his wit as a weapon against the upper classes, and of Harpo's antic charm and the fact that he was oddly sexy — he grabs women, pulls their skirts off and gets away with it.' *(It was a different era before you have a go at me!)*

Ramis worked in a mental institution in St. Louis, which he said gave him good training to help him deal with people who had anxiety, grief and even rage.

Ramis's writing skills got him a job for Playbook magazine as sole editor.

He also worked with John Belushi, and it was John who got Ramis to work in New York on 'The National Lampoon Radio Hour.'

Between 1976-1979, he performed on and was a head writer for 'Saturday Night Live'.

Harold's Famous quotes:

'I never work just to work. It's some combination of laziness and self-respect.'

'No matter what I have to say. I'm still trying to say it in a comedic form.'

Richard Belzer 1944 -

Richard Belzer was an American stand-up comedian, author and actor born in Bridgeport, Connecticut, in 1944. It is said (by him) that he was thrown out or asked to leave every school he attended 'due to uncontrollable wit'.

After doing various jobs alongside other stand-ups and after a divorce, Belzer relocated to New York City. He worked as a stand-up comic in Pips, The Improv, and Catch a Rising Star. Belzer was also part of a comedy group that satirised TV, which eventually became the film 'The Groove Tube.'

He once sued Hulk Hogan for dropping him on his head! 'The Belz', as he was known, had a reputation of being a bit of a cynic in the entertainment industry.

Between 1975-1980 Belzer was a warmup comic for 'Saturday Night Live'. During the 1970s, he was also a regular on the 'Howard Stern Show'. From 1973–1975 he worked on The National Lampoon Radio Hour; Belzer was a player alongside such comedy stars, including John Belushi, Chevy Chase, Bill Murray, Gilda Radner and Harold Ramis.

Belzer was also part of several Comedy Central 'Friars Club' roasts. He also hosted a six-part comedy special for

Cinemax called 'The Richard Belzer Show. Belzer also wrote a book, 'How to be a stand-up comic'.

In the '90s, Belzer appeared in many TV shows, including 'The Flash,' 'Lois and Clark,' and 'The New Adventures of Superman.' Following this, his main TV exposure was as a police detective in 'Homicide: Life on the Street' (1993-99) and 'Law and Order: Special Victims Unit' (1999 -2013)

Richard's Famous quotes:

'If you tell a lie that's big enough and you tell it often enough, people will believe you're telling the truth, even if what you're saying is total crap.'

'The truth will set you free...unless you want to know the truth about who killed JFK.'

'I've known Chevy Chase for so long. I actually knew him when he was funny.'

'My grandmother was very funny. It skipped a generation.'

'I went to several public schools. I went to a religious school. I was thrown out of Hebrew school, which was the final straw. They said, 'Gd doesn't like you anymore. Go eat pork.''

Belzer had what he called 'Never-to-fail' responses to hecklers, which included:

'This is what happens when a fetus doesn't get enough oxygen, ladies and gentlemen.'
'What do you use for birth control – your personality?'
'If I want any more shit from you, I'll squeeze your head.'
'Sir, I have a mike, you have a beer, gd has a plan – and you're not in it.'

Henry Churniavsky's insight into a bit of bacon

I remember being brought up with 'no bacon'. The reason is a pig has a cloven hoof. So, we can't eat it. So, I hit on the idea of a paraplegic pig! Issue solved. It's very difficult to get (have you tried to find it?) I looked at eBay and Amazon; there is not much call I can tell you. Then one day, I found something on eBay. I was bidding for it, but I think a rabbi was also trying. I won; however, it was disappointing, to be honest, ...it was not a paraplegic pig but a plastic pig – but, hey, that's my dyslexia for you.

1945

Gabe Kaplan 1945 –

Gabe Kaplan is an American comedian, actor and pro poker player! He was born in Brooklyn, New York, in 1945. After realising he would not be a Major League Baseball Player *(He is Jewish, right, baseball and Jewish don't mix)*, he looked for other interests and began working as a bellman at Lakewood, New Jersey. He found comedians staying in the hotel and eventually got to perform there. This was the start of his short stand-up career.

In 1964 he developed his stage routine at the Café Tel Aviv in NYC.

He found early success and toured the country. His act was based on his childhood experiences.

Kaplan also appeared on 'The Tonight Show' with Johnny Carson from May 1973 – Dec 1974. His act comprised a version of 'The Dating Game' with old people, and he used the line, 'I lived in Miami for a while, in a section with a lot of really old people. The average age in my apartment house was dead.'

He also at this time recorded a comedy album, 'Holes and Mello-Rolls', from which he got the catchphrase, 'Up your hole with a Mello-Roll' and included routines about his high school days.

Kaplan was well-known on television for the sitcom 'Welcome Back, Kotter'.

After the sitcom, he continued with stand-up and was in several movies, including 'Fast Break' (1978), and he portrayed Groucho Marx in a one-person show.

By 1978 Kaplan had started his poker career, and by 1980 was considered one of the best in his field; he continued until 2007.

Kaplan still does stand -up and has worked on adaptations of his sitcom.

Henry Churniavsky's insight into (some) childhood experiences

I remember great times when I stayed over with friends. I remember one time when I was eight, and after a good sleep, eventually, my best friend Andy and I chatted for hours. It must have gone 10 pm before we fell asleep (Hey, I was used to being in bed making no noise at 5.30 pm! Don't judge), and the following morning we were woken up my friend's older brother, Joe, he advised us when asking for breakfast to follow his lead! We went downstairs to have breakfast, ready to follow Joe. As we entered the room, Andy's mum called out, 'Joe, what do you want for breakfast?'

'Co-Co Pops, bitch!'

She swung around and belted him (yes, in days gone by, mothers did hit their children, and we survived...ok, though we need psychiatric support now).

Andy's mum looked at me and said, 'Sorry, Henry, what would you like?'

I replied, 'I'm definitely not asking for fucking co-co pops now.'

1946

Gilda Radner 1946 - 1989

Gilda Radner was an American comedian and actress; she was born in Detroit, Michigan, in 1946. She was one of the seven original cast members on NNC 'Saturday Night Live'. Radner specialised in parodies of TV stereotypes, especially newsreaders. She won an Emmy for her performances on the show and was famous for her zany, larger-than-life characters. Radner was referred to as 'The Sweetheart of American Comedy'.

Radner's parents, Henrietta and Herman Radner, were a big influence on her. She was very close to her father, who ran a hotel in Detroit, and he introduced her to Broadway by taking her to see shows in New York.

Her early career took her to Toronto as she followed her then-boyfriend and got her first professional engagement on 'Godspell' In 1972. Later she joined the famous 'The Second City' comedy troupe.In 1974 and 1975, she featured on 'The National Lampoon Radio Hour' alongside such names as John Belushi, Chevy Chase, Richard Belzer, Bill Murray and Rhonda Coullet. Her big break came in 1975 as an original in the 'Not Ready for Prime-Time Players' where she first performed and then co-wrote some of the material.

Between 1975 and 1980, Radner created many obnoxious characters, making fun of newsreaders (characters included Rosanne, Roseannadanna and Baba Wawa). She also introduced an act called Emily Litella, which was an elderly creation who was hard of hearing and liked to give out angry and wrong advice.

1979, saw Radner in her one-woman show on Broadway, 'Gilda Radner- Live from New York.' The material in her show, which would never have got on TV, let her use different material with songs such as 'Lets talk dirty to the animals.' The show was later filmed by comedian Mike Nichols and released as 'Gilda Live' in 1980.

In 1980 She worked with Sam Waterston in the play 'Lunch Hour', which ran for seven months.

Radner married Gene Wilder (later to work with him on Woman in Red) and unfortunately died young with Ovarian Cancer in 1989.

Gilda's Famous quotes:

'I base most of my fashion taste on what doesn't itch.'

'I can always be distracted by love, but eventually, I get horny for my creativity.'

'Dreams are like paper; they tear so easily.'

'Adopted kids are such a pain...you have to teach them to look like you.'

Gilda as Rhonda Weiss (a Jewish American Princess) 'You don't have to be Jewish to wear Jewish jeans. But it wouldn't hurt.'

Henry Churniavsky's insight into his own princess, his daughter and her wedding

First, can I say about weddings – I hate people who say to me, "Oh, yes, I did my wedding on a shoestring!" All I can say is f*** you. You have not had to arrange a Jewish wedding, especially a Jewish Princess!

My daughter got married a few years ago now. Bridezilla, as she was fondly known. This is a fact as I looked up Bridezilla in the dictionary, and her photo was in there.

My daughter was born desperate to get married. She planned this wedding for over six years. She knew the venue, the dress, the ring, the flowers, the invites...all she needed was some poor shmuck (I don't mean it, he may read this, we love him) to marry her. He was the last piece of the jigsaw...he never saw it coming, the poor boy.

Let me take you back, briefly, to eight years before they got engaged. My Bridezilla, sorry, daughter, had been seeing this young Jewish man at Leeds University. They had been seeing each other for six months on campus, and now she was bringing him home for the weekend. So, for the first time, my wife and I were going to meet him. I had been warned by both my daughter and my wife to behave, from approximately three weeks before the event, every day!

They arrived on a Friday evening, and my daughter never left his side the whole time. The only time he was alone was when he went to the spare room to sleep. YES! The spare room. He's not getting action in my house if I'm not! I was unable to have a 'chat' with him at all, even watching a live football game on TV; my daughter sat by his side and gave me constant glares.

Eventually, on Sunday evening, he had to go and move his car - my chance for a 'chat'. I walked up to him, and I said, "I can see you think a lot of my daughter; I like that. BUT if you upset her, in any way, I will break your legs, do you understand me?"

I remember the nervous smile and the spluttering reply, "Oh, don't worry, Mr Churney, I will look after her, don't worry," as he ran back into the house.

I think a few months later in the summer, my daughter was going to America with him, so as I had not seen him again, surprise, surprise, I sent him a friendly text. "Hi. Please look after my daughter with your life, or it will be yours; best regards, The Godfather." I wanted to add a bit of humour but also make a point. Well, I think the shock of my actions or behaviour, if you like, meant he would never finish with her, but he was too scared to marry her…eight years it took him.

Gilda talked a lot about Jewish princesses, which reminded me of an old Jewish joke on mothers and daughters:

A married daughter rings her mother, 'Hello, Mama?'
'Shirley, darling, what's the matter?'
'Oh, Mama, I don't know where to begin. Both the kids are sick with the flu. The fridge has broken down, the sink is leaking, and in four hours, my Hadassah Group is coming over for lunch. What am I going to do, Mama?'
'Shirley, darling, don't worry, Mama is here. I'm going to get on the bus and get into the city. From there, I will take the train out to Long Island. On the two-mile walk to your house, I will pick up some food and cook a nice lunch for the ladies. Then I will look after the kindererlers. I'll even cook a meal for Barry for when he gets home.'
'Mama, who is Barry?'
'Barry...Barry, your husband.'
'But Mama, my husband, is called Steve...is this 555-53605?'
'No, this is 555-53650.'
'Oh...does this mean you're not coming?'

1947

Larry David 1947 –

Laurence Gene David was born in Brooklyn, New York. He is an American comedian, writer, actor, director and television producer. David is most famous to most for creating 'Seinfeld' with Jerry Seinfeld, and the HBO series 'Curb your Enthusiasm' (1999 - present-day).

Larry's parents were Rose and Mortimer Julius 'Morty' David. Morty was a men's clothing manufacturer. Morty's family came from Germany, his mother from a Polish-Jewish family (now Ukraine).

After graduating, David went to the University of Maryland and got a Bachelor's Degree in History. He later enlisted in the United States Army Reserve.

It was while he was at college David started to develop his comedy as he realised that he made people laugh by just being himself *(just watch Curb!)*. While based in Manhattan, he worked on his stand-up and did several day jobs. Later he became a writer and a member of the cast for ABC's 'Friday' (1980-1982) and a writer for NBC 'Saturday Night Live' (1984-1985).

In 1989, David teamed up with Jerry Seinfeld to create 'Seinfeld', which became one of the most successful shows in history. It was for this show that Seinfeld was nominated 19 times for an Emmy, of which he won twice. One for best comedy and one for writing.

1999 was the start of 'Curb your Enthusiasm' with a one-hour special. A TV series followed a year later, which is still in production. David had the idea of making this an improv show; he would only give the actors a story outline and only a few pages of script.

David and friends made a mock documentary about Larry David and a return to stand-up for a one-off special on HBO. The final show, as in pure LD way, never materialised; however, a mock documentary did catch David doing small stand-up gigs in small venues, which can only be classed as 'The LD way.'

Not only did Larry David produce two incredible shows, he also wrote and directed the film 'Sour Grapes' (1998). David has also had various cameo roles in a number of shows, and in 2013 he co-wrote and starred in the HBO TV film 'Clear History'.

David also produced a Broadway hit, 'Fish in the Dark' (2015), and at the time, the show broke all box office records for advance sales.

David's Famous quotes:

'Women love a self-confident bald man.'

'Prett-ay, Prett-ay, Prett-ay good.'

'Trying on pants is one of the most humiliating things a man can suffer that doesn't involve a woman.'

'If you tell the truth about how you're feeling, it becomes funny.'

'I was planning my future as a homeless person. I had a really good spot picked out.'

'I tolerate lactose like I tolerate people.'

'The addition of nuts in salad...I always find it to be beneficial.' ...' I'm anti-cheese in salad.'

'I don't like to be out of my comfort zone, which is about half an inch wide.'

'A date is an experience you have with another person that makes you appreciate being alone.'

'It was supposed to say, 'Beloved Aunt', Not 'Beloved C**t.'

'Smile! - Hey, mind your own business, how about that?'

'He wanted to do a 'stop and chat'; I didn't want to do a 'stop and chat'.

'The lunch in a normal American restaurant is very problematic for me. I don't like to have hot food for lunch.'

'There's also a certain rhythm to the way Jews talk that might be funny.'

'If I tried to flirt with a woman and she didn't know who I was, she would run away.'

Henry Churniavsky's insight into relationships with a girlfriend

Larry's comment reminded me of my first romantic weekend away with a girl I had been seeing for a while. I was in my early 20s, and I wanted to take, let's call her, Sophie (to protect the innocent, well she wasn't that innocent I can tell you, sorry Sophie if you have realised who this is).

At the time, my dad owned a small boat (I say boat, more a cabin cruiser which could sleep 6) on the lakes at Bowness in the Lake District (yes, I know, I'm a spoilt young Jewish boy, get over it).

I asked my dad if I could use the boat and stay over for a few nights with the new girlfriend. He was fine about it, and I gave him the dates and reminded him a few days later.

The issue with my dad is that he was a bit like the absent-minded professor and never really thought about *long term consequences or situations of how things were done; he would do his own thing most of the time. 'No, no, go and enjoy yourself, when? Oh, yes, this weekend. Ok, yes, go and enjoy,' were the last words we spoke before the weekend.*

It was great. We arrived Friday afternoon, had sex, went out for dinner, came back, more sex (my kids will hate this story; I can feel their disapproval). I was not allowed a life before marriage to their mother.

Saturday morning, afternoon and evening sex (I know what a stud!), we were having a great time without any care in the world. Sunday morning, we woke up, and yes again (hey, we lived with our parents, so getting quality time together was limited!). The next thing I realised is the boat is rocking more than normal; I did assume I was on the top of my game at this point, but NO! I hear voices coming from the upstairs deck! Known voices. I was like a Meerkat trying to look outside while still semi-naked. WTF! It is my dad. OMG, could it get any worse – oh, yes, it could; he has brought his mother, MY grandmother, to the Lakes for a day out and to join us. REALLY, DAD? REALLY? Bear in mind no one has met 'what's her name?' Oh, yes, Sophie yet.

Now my grandmother is asking questions (loudly, like all grandparents who seem to think because she can't hear, no one else can), 'My bubele.' (That's a Jewish term of endearment) 'Vay are you only in your gatkas?' (Yiddish for underpants), 'Oh, and who is the semi-naked young lady behind you?'

I gave my dad such a look, and all he could say is, 'Oh, I thought we would come and join you for the day!' Really? My first dirty weekend away with a girl, and there are four of us!

Albert Brooks 1947

Albert Lawrence Einstein Brooks was born in Beverley Hills, California, in 1947. An American actor, comedian, writer and director. Brooks was a poet of neurosis, a unique comedic voice of the late 20th century. His stand-up career was only short, but his recordings were ground-breaking and pushed the boundaries.

Brooks' father was a radio comedian, Harry Einstein. His mother, Thelma, was a singer and actress. You could say show business was in his blood. After dropping out of Carnegie Mellon University, where Brooks studied drama, he started to do stand-up in 1968 and, at 19, changed his name from Einstein to Brooks *(to avoid confusion, I am sure)*.

In the 1960s, he was a regular on variety and talk shows, making his national debut on the 'Steve Allen Show'. He also was a regular on the 'Dean Martin Show'. In 1975 Brooks directed six short films for NBC's 'Saturday Night Live'. These six films all had a special host for each episode which included George Carlin, Paul Simon, Rob Reiner, Candice Bergen, Richard Pryor, Elliott Gould.

Brooks led a new generation of 'self-reflective' comics, and he performed on 'Ed Sullivan', 'The Tonight Show with Johnny Carson' and the 'Merv Griffin Show'. He even opened for Neil Diamond and Richie Havens.

Brook's egotistical, narcissistic, nervous comedy was an influence on comics such as Steve Martin and Andy Kaufman.

Comedy Albums such as 'Comedy Minus One'. (1973) and the Grammy Award nomination 'A Star is Bought' (1975).

Brooks' career in films include 'Taxi Driver' (his debut), 'Private Benjamin', 'Modern Romance', 'Broadcast News' for which he received an Academy Award Nomination for Best Supporting Actor, 'Finding Nemo', 'Drive', and in 2017, 'I Love You, Daddy'. He also appeared on the TV shows 'The Odd Couple' and 'The Simpsons' (1990-2015).

Albert's Famous quotes:

'If we had three million exhibitionists and one voyeur, nobody could make any money.'

'I was in Kashmir last weekend. Went to visit one of my sweaters.'

'It's interesting when your part of a group…The Jews, to be exact…that the world has had such problems with.'

'I, sort of, got into comedy accidentally, and it got bigger than I wanted it to.'

'When I die, if the word 'thong' appears in the first or second sentence of my obituary. I've screwed up.'

Albert talked about obituaries/death, which reminded me of an old Jewish joke from the Yiddish theatre.

'Ladies and gentlemen,' the manager announces, 'I am terribly sorry to have to tell you that the great actor Yizhak Cohen has had a fatal stroke in his dressing room a short time ago, and we cannot go on with tonight's performance.'

A woman in the stalls shouts, 'Quick, give him an enema.'

'Lady,' shouts the manager, 'the stroke was fatal.'

'So, give him an enema,' shouts the lady.

'Lady, you don't understand. Yizhak is dead; an enema can't possibly help.'

'Vell,' she replies, 'It wouldn't hurt.'

Richard Lewis 1947 -

Richard Philip Lewis was born in Brooklyn, New York, in 1947. He was an American self-deprecating comedian and actor who found fame in the 1980s and then turned to acting. Starring in the sitcoms 'Anything but Love' (1989-1992) and 'Curb Your Enthusiasm' (2000 - present-day).

Richard's father was a caterer and his mother an actress. It is said that Lewis, when asked about being raised in New Jersey, once said, 'I was lowered in New Jersey.' He did also say, 'I was raised by wolves.' A reference to not seeing much of his father, who died young and having a mother who 'didn't get me.'

Lewis recalls that in his early days, he was the class clown, and in the 1970s, he started his stand-up career as well as keeping a day job as a copywriter. He was also writing comedy for Playboy.

He and Larry David, as teenagers, were arch-rivals at summer camp and (born only three days apart in the same hospital), at the time Lewis hated Larry for being obnoxious. Still, later they met up as comedians in New York and became friends.

During the 1980s, he appeared on 'Late Night with David Letterman' and on his own television specials on HBO. His 'shtick' was that he was always dressed in black.

His acting debut was in 'Diary of a Young Comic'. He also co-starred with Jamie Lee Curtis in the TV Sitcom 'Anything but Love' and with Don Rickles on 'Daddy Dearest'.

Lewis made much of his psychological troubles. Mel Brooks once said, 'he may just be the Franz Kafka of modern comedy.' (Kafka was a German-speaking novelist and short story writer, regarded as one of the major figures of the 20th century literature) Lewis regards his act as a form of therapy.

Lewis once persuaded Larry David to visit his shrink. During the group discussion, David had enough and decided to leave, saying they were all insane. Lewis decided to get him back and, with the other 10 'neurotics', chased him down the road. Davis ran to a telephone phone box and would not come out until they all left him alone!

He achieved a ranking of #45 on Comedy Central's list of '100 Greatest Stand-Ups of All Time'. He also claims to be the originator of the phrase 'The ... From Hell', which in 'Curb' is brought up in a very funny episode.

Richard's Famous quotes:

'I quit therapy because my analyst was trying to help me behind my back.'

'My mother wanted to come tonight, but I would not let her...she has gossip dyslexia...she talks in front of people's backs.'

'When you're in love, it's the most glorious two and half days of your life.'

'My act is always a work in progress. I pray I have a bad day before a show.'

'My performance level has risen – my anxiety levels have skyrocketed.'

'Most Texans think Hanukkah is some sort of duck call.'

'My grandmother was a Jewish juggler. She used to worry about six things at once.'

Henry Churniavsky's insight into relationships with Grandmothers

You always know when your grandmother cooks for the family, it's going to be good, and you can never refuse. To refuse is a deadly sin, as all she will say is, 'You are refusing a bit more of my food. Gd, forbid he hears dis! Do you know how long I have slaved, yes, slaved in the kitchen to make dis meal...not two or three hours but five hours of my life, but that's not important, I do it for love, now more latkas.'

Henry Churniavsky's* insight *into relationships with Hanukkah

Chanukah/Hanukkah. *How do you explain a Jewish Holiday where you light candles because 1,000 years ago, the Jewish people were running out of oil for the Everlasting Light? And a miracle happened as the light lasted eight days until they got more oil. The way I explain it to Gentiles is easy. Imagine your mobile phone is on 5% battery, you have lost your charger, but you need to use the phone until a new charger arrives in the post eight days later. The phone works for eight days with a small amount of juice in the battery until your new charger arrives. A miracle!*

1948

Lewis Black 1948

Lewis Niles Black, born in Washington D.C. in 1948, is an American stand-up comedian, author, playwright, social critic and actor. He is mainly known for his angry demeanour and belligerent style, and he is obsessed with human stupidity! His routine covers history, politics and religion.

Lewis's mother, Jeannette, was a teacher, and his father, Sam, was an artist and mechanical engineer. Lewis was brought up in a middle-class Jewish family in Maryland, and he graduated in 1966.

Black studied playwriting at the University of North Carolina, and upon graduating in 1970, he went back home to Washington, where he wrote plays and performed stand-up at The Brickskeller in Dupont Circle.

Black's career began in theatre as a playwright; he said that stand-up was something that he 'did on the side'. Between 1981-1989 he wrote numerous plays, but he would do his stand-up as an opening act for the plays. He was also the MC of events. His stand-up got him appearances on the 'Late Show' with David Letterman and Conan O'Brien.

In 1998, Black starred in his first comedy special on 'Comedy Central Presents.' Two more specials followed in 2000 and 2002. The special in 2002 was entitled 'Taxed Beyond Belief'.

His first CD in 2000, 'The White Album', took its art design from the Beatles album. In 2001, he appeared in the one-person show – 'Black Humour' in New York City, and in 2002, he released the 'Revolver' EP, followed by the CD 'Rules of Enragement' in 2003. Black hosted the 'World Stupidity Awards' in Canada in 2004 and 2005, for the 'Just for Laughs Festival'.

He appeared in the HBO TV Special 'Black on Broadway' in 2004, and in 2005 appeared at the Luther Burbank Performing Arts Centre.

In 2006, Black performed at Warner Theatre in Washington in HBO's 'Red, White and Screwed' and went on to perform at Carnegie Hall in 2006.

By 2008, he released the CD 'Anticipation' and hosted a 2-hour comedy documentary on the 'History of the Joke'. He also presented some of Comedy Central's 'Stand-up Month' specials. Black's routine got him to #5 on 'Stand-up Showdown 2008' and #11 in 2010. Another CD followed in 2010, 'Stark Raving Black.' He also toured with his book 'Me of Little Faith'.

In 2011, Black filmed two shows in Minneapolis. These shows were used for Black's comedy special 'In Gd We Rust'. Comedy Central also released live recordings from the 1990 'The Prophet' and 'In Gd We Rust.'

In the 2015 animated movie 'Inside Out' Black was the voice of Anger (*who else?*). Then in 2017, he released a new CD, 'Black to the Future' and 'The Rant Is Due'.

Black also created the Carolina comedy festival. Black has appeared in several films from 1986 – 2019, including 'Hannah and her Sisters' (Woody Allen), 'The Night We Never Met', 'Peep World' and many more. He has appeared on a variety of TV shows, such as 'Law and Order', 'Mad About You', and 'Homicide'; even video games have the Black touch. He has authored over 40 plays.

Lewis's Famous quotes:

'There's no such thing as soy milk. It's soy juice.'

'Republicans have nothing but bad ideas, and Democrats have no idea.'

'It's absolutely stupid that we live without an ozone layer. We have men; we've got rockets, we've got saran wrap – fix it.'

'What I find most disturbing about Valentine's Day is, look, I get that you have to have a holiday of love, but in the height of the flu season, it makes no sense.'

'Do you know what 'meteorologist' means in English? It means liar.'

'You've got to be stupid to heckle me – I am very equipped to win.'

'Every time I use an app, part of my brain dies! We'll get to the point where we go to bed and wonder: 'Did I have a thought today? You'll have to go to your 'Thought' app!'

'Parenting isn't just parenting your own child.'

'If you're working out in front of a mirror and watching your muscles grow, your ego has reached a point where it is now eating itself. That's why I believe there should be a psychiatrist at every health club so that when they see you doing this, they will take you away for a little chat.'

Lewis talked about getting parenting. So, I have added an old Jewish joke on the subject:

Little Sam was shopping with his mum, something he didn't like very much. But as he passed a toy shop, he sprung to life. He saw a toy he really wanted. Sam begged his mum, but she refused every time he asked. He got so rude that his mother firmly said, 'I'm very sorry, Sam, but we did not come out today to buy you a toy.'

Sam turned angrily and said, 'I've never met a woman as horrible as you.'

Holding his hand gently, she replied, 'Sam, darling, one day you'll get married and then you will, you really will, I promise you.'

Henry Churniavsky's insight *into working out and sport*

Jews are no good at sport. Fact! Well, maybe Jew Jitsu.

I've just found the best machine in the gym. It does my biceps, my squats, my stomach, all in one machine. It's called the vending machine.

Billy Crystal 1948 -

William Edward Crystal was born in Manhattan in 1948, moving later to New York. Crystal is an American actor, comedian, singer, writer, producer, director and television host *(Oy, a busy boy!)*. He gained attention in the 1970s in *(one of my favourite comedies programmes in this era)* 'Soap.' Crystal became a global Hollywood star doing films such as 'The Princess Bride', 'Throw Momma from the Train' (both 1987), 'When Harry met Sally' (1989), 'City Slickers' (1991), 'Mr Saturday Night' (1992) which Crystal wrote, directed and starred, and 'Forget Paris' (1995). Crystal also starred alongside Robert De Niro in 'Analyze This' (1999), and in 2020 he was working on 'Monsters at Work' for Disney.

Billy's family consisted of him, two older brothers, his mother Helen, a housewife and his father Jack, who owned and worked the Commodore Music Store (which was founded by Helen's father). Jack was also musical; he was a jazz promoter and was also an executive of the jazz record label Commodore Records, which was founded by Helen's brother. Crystal's family came from Austria and Russia.

From an early age, comedy was in his blood. He and his brothers would do comedy routines from comics such as Bob Newhart, Rich Little and Sid Caesar. After graduating, Crystal attended Marshall University in West Virginia on a baseball scholarship, but it never came to fruition as the team became defunct. Crystal eventually returned to New York City and transferred to NYU, where he studied film and television under Martin Scorsese and graduated in 1970 with a B.F.A.

For a few years, he was part of a comedy trio, playing colleges and gigs and perfecting his impressions, while at the same time, he was a substitute teacher during the day.

During the mid-1970s, he moved to California as a solo act and worked at The Improv and Catch a Rising Star. It was at this time the Comedy Store director Norman Lear spotted Crystal and managed to get Crystal to fill in at 'The Dean Martin Celebrity Roast of Muhammad Ali', which got him a lot of good publicity.

In 1976 Crystal appeared in an episode of 'All in the Family', and in 1977, he got his big break on the American television series 'Soap', which ran for an impressive four years until 1981, playing Jodie Dallas, one of the first openly gay characters ever seen on Television.

In 1978 Crystal had his first film role with Joan Rivers in 'Rabbit Test'. By 1982 Crystal was starting to host his own variety shows, and 'The Billy Crystal Comedy Hour' was on NBC, but this was cut short after a few shows. He hosted 'Saturday Night Live' where he would do a sketch about being a talk show host (impression of Fernando

Lamas), and his catchphrase 'You look…mahvelous!' became his schtick.

Due to the success of his stand-up and Saturday Night Live, Crystal released an album of stand-up material 'Mahvelous' in 1985. This album was nominated for a Grammy for best comedy recording in 1986.

Crystal has hosted The Academy Awards nine times. He won the award in 1989 and 1991 for the Best Individual Performance in a Variety or Music programme. He won a Tony award in 2005 for his show '700 Sundays'. A two-act one-man play which is based on his parents and his childhood. Crystal has also been nominated 12 times for an Emmy and won it three times. He has hosted and co-directed The Comic Relief Festival since 1986.

In 2013 Crystal brought a show to Broadway for two months at the Imperial Theatre, which HBO filmed for a 2014 special. He also won a Grammy in 2014 for the 'Best-Spoken Word Album'. Crystal has also written a number of books, including '700 Sundays'.

Crystal was a one-woman man. His wife, Janice, was his first and only date. It was reported that on one occasion, Crystal was with his assistant in Chicago, and every room in every hotel in the city was booked. They found a twin room, and they had to share it. Lacy (his assistant) tried to make a pass at Crystal during the night by saying she was cold. Crystal replied, 'How would you like to be Mrs Crystal for the night?'

Lacy was excited, 'I'd love to be Mrs Crystal for the night.'

Crystal replied, 'Then get up and shut the window then!'

Billy's Famous quotes:

'I'm comfortable being old...being black...being Jewish.'

'I still don't love the darkness, though I've learned to smile in it a little bit, now and then.'

'Your success is in your point of view. It's your life that you're talking about; it's your observations. That's the best lesson that I ever had.'

'Gentlemen, start your ego's.'

'To be good, you need to believe in what you're doing.'

'My grandparents invented joylessness. They were not fun. I've already had more fun with my grandchildren than my grandparents ever had with me.'

'I'm a baby. I sleep like a baby – I'm up every two hours. And I think a lot. I worry a lot. I have great nights of no sleep where ideas come.'

'Women need a reason to have sex. Men just need a room.'

Crystal talked a lot in his sets about marriage. So here is an old Jewish Joke on that subject

A couple was preparing to get married and met up with their rabbi for their final session. The rabbi asked if they had any questions.
The man says, 'Is it true men and women don't dance together?'
The rabbi said, 'Yes, for modest reasons, men and women dance separately.'
'So, I can't dance with my own wife?'
'No.'
'Ok, but what about sex?'
'Well, that's fine,' says the rabbi. 'It's a mitzvah within the marriage.'
'What about different positions?'
'No problem.' Says the rabbi.
'Woman on top?' says the man.
'Vay no.' replies the rabbi.
'What about standing up?'
'No,' says the rabbi. 'That could lead to dancing.'

Billy talked about getting grandparents. So, I have added an old Jewish joke on the subject:

It was David's third birthday party, and he was having so much fun. At the end, it was time to open his presents. One was from his grandma Bubie; in it was a water pistol. He was so excited, jumping up and down, and Bubie helped to fill the pistol with water.

David's mother saw this and was not best pleased. She turned to her mother and said, 'Mom, I'm surprised at you. Don't you remember how we used to drive you meshuga (mad) with water pistols when we were young?'

Bubie smiled and replied, 'I remember. Of course, I remember.'

Crystal talked about parenting and growing up in a play he produced. So, a bit more form Henry Churniavsky:

In 2020, I produced a solo show, 'Aaaah, I'm Jewrotic, and I blame my Jewish Mother…Who Else? Here are a few clips to enjoy (hopefully).

My mother, despite the need for sleep, taught me many things in my early life. Some things I will never forget. She taught me:

Religion: 'You better pray that stain will come out of the carpet. Or you will wish you were never born.'

Time travel: *'If you don't behave, I'm going to knock you into the middle of next week!'*
My reply to this was, 'I wish you would; I'm having a bloody awful week this week.'

Logic: 'Because I said so, that's why.'

Irony: 'Stop crying, or I will give you something to cry about.'

Hypocrisy: 'If I've told you once, I've told you a million times...don't exaggerate.'

Envy: 'There are millions of less fortunate children in this world who don't have wonderful parents like you do.'

As a child, I remember getting a bead stuck up my nose. My mum could not get it out, so she rushed me to A&E. The nurse said, 'I will show what to do in the future - if he tries this again.'
I remember my mum would put her mouth over mine, press my nose on the side opposite to where the bead was stuck, and she would blow. It caused not only the bead to fly out, but also give me nightmares of my mum French kissing me!!! I remember my first real girlfriend who tried to kiss me with her mouth open; I screamed, 'FFS, I don't have any beads up my nose!'

1949

Andy Kaufman 1949 – 1984

Andrew Geoffrey Kaufman was born in New York City in 1949. An American entertainer, actor, wrestler and performance artist, Kaufman, was often seen as a comedian, but he preferred the term 'song and dance man'. Andy was the oldest of three children to Janice, a housewife and ex-fashion model and Stanley Kaufman, a jewellery salesman.

Kaufman started to perform at an early age performing at children's parties at nine years old. He used to like writing stories and poetry. After graduating, he studied television production at Grahm Junior College in Boston, where he starred in his own campus television show, 'Uncle Andy's Funhouse'.

In 1969 he went to Las Vegas and performed at coffee houses, developing his act, but he also wrote a one-person play, 'Gosh'. After graduating in 1971, he began performing stand-up comedy around the East Coast.

Kaufman started to receive attention when he started character comedy. His character was 'Foreign Man', and he managed to convince Budd Friedman at New York's, The Improv comedy club to let him try out this character to an audience. Kaufman was a unique comedian; he would come on stage to a recording from the Mighty

Mouse cartoon playing and just stare at the audience; he would then lip-sync one line, 'Here I come to save the day'. After that, he would purposely tell a few bad jokes and then conclude in this meek, high pitched, heavily accented voice some celebrity impersonations. The joke being he was so bad at it. One of his impressions would be Elvis Presley. This act got Kaufman onto the first season of 'Saturday Night Live'. This character was later to be re-named Latka and was introduced to a new comedy sitcom 'Taxi' *(Again, this is a must-see comedy programme that catapulted many stars to bigger things, including Danny De Vito and Judd Hirsch)*. Kaufman was a unique character who was able to use his personality to do various, and random other characters like his alter ego, Tony Clifton.

'Taxi' ran from 1978–1983 but during this time, Kaufman continued to tour clubs and theatres, sometimes as himself or the obnoxious lounge singer Tony Clifton. He appeared on sketch shows, and late night talk shows, in particular, 'Late Night with David Letterman'.

In 1979 Kaufman performed at New York's Carnegie Hall. He invited his 'grandmother' to the show and had a chair placed at the side of the stage so everyone could see her. At the end of the show, she stood up, took her mask off to reveal the comedian Robin Williams.

This performance was also noted for two other facts; one is that he had an elderly woman pretend to have a heart attack and die on stage, and he would dance over her to revive her, and at the end of the show, the audience were taken in buses, out for milk and cookies.

This was not a one-off; his behaviour was often bizarre. Here are a few things Kaufman subjected his audiences to in his short career; eating raw potatoes onstage for no apparent reason. Acting as a hopeless foreign comic before going into an Elvis routine.

In 1978 he launched a College Sex Concert Tour; the primary purpose was to help him bed young girls who sent him fan mail.

He started the Inter-gender Wrestling Championship. He would offer $1,000 to any woman who could pin him down. 1979 also saw a TV special based on his junior college idea 'Andy's Funhouse'.

In 1981 Kaufman made three appearances on 'Fridays', a variety show. In one sketch, a brawl ensued due to issues on set. First, Kaufman refused to speak, a cast member went off stage to return with cue cards and threw them on the table; Kaufman responded by splashing him with water and then the co-producer, Jack Burns, stormed on to the stage, and the brawl ensued. Then it cut to a commercial break.

Kaufman even had his professional wrestling act come into 'The Letterman Show', as this became a big part of his very short life.

Unfortunately, at 35 years old, Andy Kaufman died of lung cancer. Due to the fact he was a massive prankster, rumours circulated at the time that he had, in fact, faked his own death. Alas, this was not true, and this robbed us of what is known as a comedy genius.

His legacy is immense. Richard Lewis, in a comedy salute to Andy Kaufman, said, 'No one has ever done what Andy did, and did it as well, and no one will ever. Because he did it first. So did Buster Keaton, so did Andy.'

Carl Reiner said, 'Did Andy influence comedy? No. Because nobody's doing what he did. Jim Carrey was influenced not to do what Andy did but to follow his own drummer. I think Andy did that for a lot of people. Follow your own drumbeat.'

In 2019 it was announced that Kaufman was to be honoured in the Hollywood Walk of Fame in the television category and will be part of the Class of 2020.

Andy's Famous quotes:

'I am not a comic; I have never told a joke...The comedian's promise is that he will go out there and make you laugh with him. My only promise is that I will try to entertain you as best I can.'

'Tank you veddy much.'

'I'm just singing a song, and if people want to laugh, that's their business.'

'I just want real reactions. I want people to laugh from the gut, be sad from the gut, or get angry from the gut.'

'There's no way to describe what I do. It's just me.'

'I'm having everything. I'm a vegetarian, too. But in my mother's house, I eat whatever I'm served.'

'I just want the audience to have a wonderful, happy feeling inside them and leave with big smiles on their faces.'

Garry Shandling 1949 – 2016

Garry Emmanuel Shandling was born in Chicago, Illinois in 1949, and grew up in Arizona. Shandling was an American stand-up comedian, actor, director, writer and producer. He is best known for 'The Garry Shandling's Show' and 'The Larry Sanders Show'. Garry had one brother. His parents were Irving, a print shop owner, and Muriel, a pet store owner.

After graduating from Palo Verde High School, Shandling attended the University of Arizona, majoring in electrical engineering. He left this course and completed a degree in marketing, followed by a postgraduate course in writing. He also sent funny articles to various magazines.

At 19, he went to Phoenix to tell some jokes to George Carlin; he made the same two-hour journey the next day, and Carlin told him to stick at it as he had something *(he drove two hours just to tell a few jokes. It reminds me of the times we all, as comics, drive, bus, train, hitchhike for hours just to do a 5-or 10-min set - yes, we are a meshuganah (mad) group of people, but we love it).*

In 1973, Shandling moved to Los Angeles and started work in an advertising agency. At the same time, he sold a script for the sitcom 'Sandford & Son.' He also wrote scripts for the sitcom 'Welcome Back, Kotter.' In the late

1970s, he teamed up with Paul Wilson to form an improv group.

After a car accident in 1977, which left him in a critical condition, he decided that once he'd recovered, he was going to pursue a career in comedy.

In 1978 Shandling did his first stand-up routine at the Comedy Store in Los Angeles. Shandling's comedy persona was an anxious, grimacing, confused man who seemed to be on the verge of losing control. He spent the next few years on the road. He even crossed a picket line at a comedy club as he so wanted to make the grade. He made a debut spot in 1981 in 'The Tonight Show Starring Johnny Carson'. Shandling did so well he eventually substituted for Carson on many occasions until 1987, which was when he left to start his cable show.

In 1984, Shandling performed his first stand-up special 'Garry Shandling: Alone in Vegas'. A second TV special followed in 1986, 'The Garry Shandling Show: 25th Anniversary Special' (for which the show was nominated for four Emmy Awards) both for 'Showtime'. The third of his specials aired in 1991, 'Garry Shandling: Stand-up'.

Shandling had a great career in television, and in 1985, with Alan Zweibel, he created the 'It's Garry Shandling's Show'. The idea for the show was to take comedy back to the era of the George Burns and Gracie Allen Show, where the characters acknowledged the audience and talked directly to them. This show won numerous awards.

The Larry Sanders Show launched in 1992; it ran for 89 episodes and was nominated for a total of 56 Emmy Awards, which it won on three occasions. During this time, while Shandling was at the height of his career, an offer was made that gave him the opportunity to take over two major shows (Late Night with David Letterman and The Late Show).

Shandling hosted the Grammy Awards on four occasions and The Emmy's twice, which he also co-hosted one year.

Shandling appeared in many films from 1993–2018, including 'Zoolander' (2001), 'Iron Man 2' (2010) and other films that were released posthumously.

Garry's Famous quotes:

'I have such poor vision I can date anybody.'

'I'm too shy to express my sexual needs except over the phone to people I don't know.'

'I once saw an elaborate landscape in a gallery, drawn in pencil, that took my breath away. Then I realised the artist probably didn't have enough confidence to use a pen.'

'There's a good chance that if you're talking to me when I'm snoring, it means I'm bored.'

'Dr Phil is hiding something; why wouldn't he use his last name?'

'I practice safe sex; I use an airbag.'

'My friends tell me I have an intimacy problem. But they don't really know me.'

'Jews don't go camping, well unless it's catered.'

'I belong to a group called sex without partners.'

'I have a mirror above my bed, and it says on it, "objects are larger than they appear." '

'People should know TV adds 4 to 5 lbs to your lips.. people say I talk about my hair a lot, and they say can't you talk about current events...sure how does my hair look right now.'

'I'm dating a woman now who, evidently, is unaware of it.'

Henry Churniavsky's insight *into dating.*

While researching for my blog, I recently went online to look at dating sites, and I realised there is so much bulls**t out there. The information women put out as what they think is right and what is actual is real. Here are some examples:

A woman will describe herself as:	What it really means for the help of the man:
40ish -	Means at least 49
Beautiful -	Pathological liar
Open-minded -	Desperate
Outgoing -	Beware; will be loud and embarrassing
Emotionally secure -	Only means on medication
Wants soul mate -	Code for a stalker

For research purposes only (you do understand, don't you darling wife! – I bet she does not get this far into the book, anyway!!) I went onto a dating website just to see how it works (honestly darling; she meant nothing!) The site I chose was one called 'Hinge'; all I can say the contact I made was unhinged.

1950

Robert Schimmel 1950 - 2010

Robert George Schimmel was born in the Bronx, New York, in 1950. He was an American stand-up comedian and known, especially, for his blue material. He is known as a 'comic's comic'.

Schimmel was the son of Otto and Betty Schimmel, who were survivors of the Holocaust. In 1980 while living in Arizona and working as a salesman, he began performing at open mic nights. He moved to Los Angeles on an offer of a regular comedy spot, but that failed to materialise as the club had burned down.

Luckily, he met Rodney Dangerfield, who gave him a spot on his HBO 'Young Comedians Special'. This is where he started to get noticed. He also began to write material for 'In Living Color' and also for comics Yakov Smirnoff and Jimmie Walker.

Schimmel used his personal life as part of his act. This included sex with his wife, masturbation, even his cancer. He was sexually explicit, so television work was difficult, but he was a hit on 'The Howard Stern Show'.

Schimmel also wrote books about his ill health, in his own humorous way: 'Cancer on Five Dollars a Day

(Chemo Not Included)' and 'How Humor Got Me Through the Toughest Journey of My Life'.

His work also included a number of albums. 'Comes Clean', 'If You buy this CD, I Can Get A Car', 'Unprotected', 'The Early Years' and 'Reserection', and videos; 'Unprotected' 'Old School' and 'Life Since Then'.

In 2004 Comedy Central had Schimmel at number 76 out of the '100 Greatest Stand-Ups of All Time'.

Robert's Famous quotes,

'I was making love one night with my wife, and she said, 'You're in me'.
'I know where I am, shut the f**k up!'

'One of my friends goes. 'So, you know what really turns me on; when girls talk dirty in bed.'
'Yeah, I tried that with my wife. I said, 'Hey, talk dirty to me.'
She said, 'Go F**k yourself.' ...Not that dirty.'

'I asked my wife to try anal sex. She said, 'Sure, you first.''

1951

Yakov Smirnoff 1951 -

Dr Yakov Naumovich Pokhis was born in Odessa, Ukraine, in 1951. Smirnoff was an art teacher in Odessa as well as doing stand-up comedy. He worked on ships on the Black Sea where he heard about America and decided this was where he wanted to go.

In 1977, he and his family eventually were able to travel to America, and he settled in New York. Despite not being able to speak English, he managed to work at the Grossinger's Hotel in the Catskill's.

In the 1980s, Smirnoff (*the name which he chose as he wanted a name the American's knew and were comfortable with*) moved to Los Angeles to do his stand-up and was a regular at the 'Comedy Store'.

Smirnoff used wordplay in his routines, based on what he learnt in America using lines such as:
'I go to New York, and I saw a big sign saying, 'America loves Smirnoff', and I said to myself, what a country.'

Upon reading a sign 'Part-Time Women Wanted.' He said, 'What a country! Even transvestites can get work.'

After getting his first film break in 1984 on the film 'Moscow on the Hudson', where he also helped Robin

Williams with the Russian dialogue, subsequent films followed; 'Brewster's Millions' (1985) and 'The Money Pit' (1986).

Smirnoff also appeared on 'The Tonight Show Starring Johnny Carson'.

In 1986-1987 he starred in the television sitcom 'What a Country', playing a Russian cab driver (*so no stereotyping there then*).

Smirnoff has entertained President Ronald Reagan, and in 1968 was the main act at the annual White House Correspondents Dinner.

Between 1993-2015 Smirnoff performed at his own 2,000 seat theatre in Branson, Missouri, which besides him performing hundreds of times a year, would feature other comedy and dance acts from native Russia.

During the late 1990s, following a divorce, he rebranded his stand-up to focus on the difference between men and women. It also included solving problems within marriage and relationships, which was his focus back in 2018 in Branson.

In 2003, he starred in the Broadway one-person show 'As Long as We Both Shall Laugh'.

After a successful career spanning tv, movies and Broadway, he began studying for a master's degree in psychology, focusing on happiness. Later in 2019, he earned a doctorate in psychology and global leadership.

Yakov's Famous quotes:

On communism: 'We have no gay people in Russia, there are homosexuals, but they are not allowed to be gay about it. The punishment is seven years locked in prison with other men, and there is a three-year waiting list for that.'

Comparing the USA with USSR.
'Here you have American Express card, 'Don't leave home without it.' In Russia, we have Russian Card - 'Don't leave home!'

'I like American women. They do things sexually Russian girls never dream of doing - like showering.'

'In Russia, we only had two TV channels. Channel One was propaganda. Channel Two consisted of a KGB officer telling you: Turn back at once to Channel One.'

'In America, you can always find a party! In Russia, Party always finds you!'

'Falling in love is a chemical reaction. But it wears off in a year.'

Henry Churniavsky's insight *into falling in love.*

I am a very lucky man (as my wife has told me on many occasions during our marriage). I married the girl of my dreams. But being a good Jewish boy, I needed my mother to approve of my choice. So, when I decided she was the one for me, I decided to play a trick on my mum and take two other female friends of mine with my beloved.

I made the girls sit on the couch and put my wife to be in the middle. I then went into the kitchen and asked my mum to come into the lounge and said, 'Mum, here are three girls, one of these I want to marry, can you guess which one?' Right away, she pointed to the one in the middle and said, 'Bet it's her.'

I was astounded. 'Wow, Mum, that's amazing; how did you know?'

Mum replied, 'Cos she's the one I don't like the look of.' That serves me right for asking (ha).

1952

Elayne Boosler 1952 -

Elayne Boosler was born to a Jewish immigrant family in 1952 and raised in Brooklyn. Her father was a Russian acrobat, and her mother a Romanian ballerina.

One of Boosler's claims to fame is that she married the former manager of the great band 'The Doors'.

Boosler started as a singer/dancer in touring companies. She met Andy Kaufman while she was a doorman at 'The Improv Club' in New York. Andy and Elayne lived together for a while, and it was Andy who persuaded her to do stand-up.

In 1986 Boosler became the first woman to get a one-hour comedy special with 'Party of One', and from this show, she toured for a year doing a two-hour comedy show.

By 2011 Boosler had done seven cable specials, which included 'Broadway Baby', 'Top Tomato' and 'Live Nude Girls'. She also had a 90-minute special on New Year's Eve, 'Elayne Boosler Midnight Hour'.

Boosler also had a television show, a game show called 'Balderdash'. Other TV work followed; 'The Late Show', 'Midnight Special', 'Comic Strip Live' and 'Friday

Night Video'. Boosler also had film credits to her name, not just for acting; she also wrote, directed and acted.

A year before Andy Kaufman's death, she and Andy wrote a special together, 'Soundstage'.

Boosler has also performed twice at the London Palladium, and she has performed for President Clinton at the White House.

Elayne's Famous quotes:

'The Vatican is against surrogate mothers. Good thing they didn't have that rule when Jesus was born.'

'You never see a man walking down the street with a woman who has a little potbelly and a bald spot.'

'My ancestors wandered lost in the wilderness for 40 years because even in biblical times, men would not stop to ask for directions.' *(This joke will be lost on the millennials with sat nav!)*

'I've never been married, but I tell people I'm divorced, so they won't think something is wrong with me.'

"I know what men want. Men want to be really, really close to someone who will leave them alone.'

'When women are depressed, they eat or go shopping. Men invade another country. It's a whole different way of thinking.'

Elayne talked about shopping. So, I have added an old Jewish joke on the subject:

Max is with his best friend Morris in his house having a drink. Morris turns to Max and comments that it's late, and his wife has not come home yet, 'Beckie is two hours late, Max,' he says.
'She's probably been kidnapped, or maybe had a crash in the car,' replies Max. 'Or maybe she's still shopping!'
'Oy Vay,' says Morris, 'I hope she's still not shopping.'

Henry Churniavsky's insight into shopping.

My wife was saying she wanted to lose weight and that she wanted an exercise bike. I told her she had one in the garage, which cost me a fortune, and it's never used. She said, 'No, I want a stationary bike.'
My response was, 'Your bike has been stationary, that's why you need to lose weight...' OOPS!

When we go shopping, I always hold her hand. Because if I let go, she shops!

I always try and please my wife. She asked me for silk for her birthday, so I went shopping...no doubt this tin of emulsion will be the wrong colour.

Alexei Sayle 1952 -

Alexei David Sayle was born in Anfield, Liverpool *(so, I'm not the only Jewish Scouse comedian!).*

Sayle is an English (Scouse) stand-up comic, actor and author. He was central to the new wave of alternative comedy in the 1980s and was voted 18th in Channel 4 's 100 greatest stand-ups in 2007. He is the son of Molly, a pools clerk and Joseph Sayle, a railway guard, both of whom were members of the Communist Party of Great Britain. Molly was of Lithuanian Jewish descent.

Alexei attended Alsop High school but did not finish the sixth form. He decided to train to become a teacher and went to Garnett College in Roehampton.

In 1979 when the Comedy Store opened in London, Sayle became its first MC (Master of Ceremonies). The Comic Strip came around in the early 1980s, and Sayle became one of the leading members of the cast. 'The Comic strip Album' (1981) and recording 'Cak' (1982). By then, Sayle had appeared on the stage and film and was part of the cast for 'The Secret Policeman's Other Ball' (1981-1982).

He is hugely political (his parents were members of the Communist Party of Great Britain), and with an angry persona, his wit and bite hit hard.

In the early years, Sayle worked on the radio at 'Capital London'. In 1979 he wrote and performed an award-winning radio series 'Alexei Sayle and the Fish People.' Later an album was released based on the show.

1982 Sayle had his first high profile television appearance on Central Independent Television with a late-night show 'O.T.T.'

Between 1982-1984 Alexei Sayle was part of comedy brilliance as he played various roles on 'The Young Ones', and between 1985-1993 he appeared in several episodes of 'The Comic Strip Presents.' Other TV series followed, 'Alexei Sayle's Stuff' (88-91), 'The All New Alexei Sayle Show' (1994-1995) and 'Alexei Sayle's Merry-Go-Round' (1998).

In 1988 Sayle took to treading the boards and appeared in Shakespeare's 'The Tempest'. Then in 1989, Sayle won an Emmy for his show 'Stuff'. In 1994 he wrote and presented 'Alexei Sayle's Liverpool', a 3-part TV series reconnecting him to his place of birth.

Sayle also was seen in various films, in serious and comedy roles. These included 'Gorky Park' (1983), Indiana Jones and the Last Crusade (1989), and in 1992, he appeared in 'Carry on Columbus'.

Sayle, throughout his career, has worked in music, and with one single, 'Ullo John! Gotta New Motor' he achieved Top 20 success in the UK (1984). He has also written a number of books, both short stories and novels.

In 1999 he wrote a five-part sitcom for the radio 'Sorry About Last Night'. In 2011, 16 years after his last stand-up, Sayle returned as an MC at the Royal Festival Hall. 2011, Saw Sayle appear in 'Nine Lessons and Carols for Godless People' at the Bloomsbury Theatre.

A full UK tour followed in 2012, which included a 16-night residency at the Soho Theatre in early 2013. He has since returned to the Edinburgh Fringe Festival and has toured in recent years with a new tour booked for 2020.

In 2016 he returned to Radio 4 with 'Alexei Sayle's Imaginary Sandwich Bar'.

Alexei's Famous quotes:

On American phrases, 'If you travel to the States, they have a lot of different words than like we use. For instance: they say 'elevator', we say 'lift'; they say 'drapes', we say 'curtains; they say 'president', we say 'seriously deranged git!'

'As a comic, you try something, and if it works, you go with it and grind it to death.'

'Dire Straits are a great band. Someone tells you they like 'Brother in Arms' and immediately you know they're a stupid annoying git.'

'Honestly, sometimes I get really fed up with my subconscious...it's like it's got a mind of its own.'

'However, my problems with my memory are further complicated by the fact that while I don't have any recollection of things I have done, I have very vivid recollections of loads of things that I haven't done.'

Henry Churniavsky's insight *into memory issues and my dad.*

When my dad developed Parkinson's and the start of dementia, he never lost his sense of humour. I remember arriving one late afternoon; I walked into the lounge, and dad was laughing to himself. I asked, 'Dad, what's so funny?'
He turned to me, showing me some medication, and he said, 'Just look at the instructions on the bottle...shake well...how else was it going to be done?'

Roseanne Barr 1952 -

Roseanne Cherrie Barr was born in Salt Lake City, Utah, in 1952. She is an American actor, comedian, writer, producer and politician. Controversy has followed her career. Barr started out as a stand-up comic before getting her most famous role, 'Roseanne', which ran from 1988 -1997 and had an ill-fated reprise in 2018.

Roseanne was the oldest of four children born to Helen, a bookkeeper and cashier and Jerome 'Jerry' Barr, who was a salesman. Her father's family were emigrants from Russia, and her maternal grandparents were from Austria-Hungary and Lithuania. On entering America, her grandfather changed the surname from 'Borisofsky' to 'Barr.'

Barr's upbringing was different. Her maternal grandmother was Orthodox Jewish, but her parents kept being Jewish a secret and were partially involved in The Church of Jesus Christ of Latter-day Saints. This led her to say, 'Friday, Saturday and Sunday morning I was a Jew; Sunday afternoon, Tuesday afternoon and Wednesday afternoon we were Mormons.'

Barr had a varied upbringing, and tribulations followed her over her career. Aged three, she contracted Bell's Palsy. In 1968 she deliberately walked into traffic, spending many days in a coma. She was later admitted to a state mental hospital for nearly a year. Barr also worked for a short stint as a prostitute. "Prostitution is a business".

In 1970, aged 18, after a troubled few years, she moved out to Colorado. She started doing stand-up gigs in Denver and Colorado; she even went to Los Angeles and tried for the Comedy Store, and in 1985 she appeared for the first time on 'The Tonight Show'.

In 1986 she performed on a Rodney Dangerfield special and on 'Late Night with David Letterman'. A year later, she got her own HBO special, 'The Roseanne Barr Show', for which she received an American Comedy Award. This led to ABC giving her own series, 'Roseanne'.

'Roseanne' was a run-away success in 1988 when the show premiered and was watched by over 21 million people (the highest debut that season). The show ran for nine seasons and won an Emmy, a Golden Globe, a Kids Choice Award and three American Comedy Awards. The final two seasons saw Barr become the second-highest-paid woman in show business (after Oprah) on (what is to be believed) $40 million.

In 1989, Barr released an autobiography, and in the same year, her film debut 'She-Devil'. Following on from that, she voiced baby Julie in 'Look Who's Talking Too'. In 1990, she courted controversy again, following an unusual rendition of 'The Star-Spangled Banner' at a baseball game.

In a 'People' magazine interview in 1991, she reported that she was physically and mentally assaulted by her parents as a child. They both denied this and passed a lie-detector test.

Between 1991 – 1994 Barr, appeared three times on 'Saturday Night Live', which she co-hosted with Tom Arnold (her ex-husband).

In 1994 she became the first female comedian to host the MTV Video Music Awards. However, it was around this time that Barr was diagnosed with many mental health disorders, including depression, obsessive compulsive disorder, acrophobia and multiple personality disorders.

In 2005 after doing various projects, she returned for a world-wide stand-up comedy tour and, in 2006, as part of her first-ever live dates in Europe, took part in the Leicester Comedy Festival in Leicester, the UK, at the De Montfort Hall.

In 2006, she appeared in the HBO comedy special 'Roseanne Barr: Blonde N Bitchin', and she headlined at the Sahara Hotel and Casino in Las Vegas in 2008. In 2014 she was a judge on 'Last Comic Standing' on NBC.

Roseanne's Famous quotes:

'Men read maps better than a woman because only men can understand the concept of an inch equalling a hundred miles.'

'Women complain about premenstrual syndrome, but I think of it as the only time of the month that I can be myself.'

'I consider myself to be a pretty good judge of people…that's why I don't like any of them.'

'Birth control that really works - every night before we go to bed, we spend an hour with our kids.'

'It's okay to be fat. So, you're fat. Just be fat and shut up.'

'Experts say you should never hit your children in anger. When is a good time? When you're feeling festive?'

Henry Churniavsky's insight into being an angry parent.

I was walking in the city centre a few weeks ago, and I was walking behind this mother who had two children. One was in the pram crying and sobbing, and the other, who was older, was playing up, as he was probably bored.

He kept running off, and his mother, who was at the end of her tether, was screaming for him to come back.

I followed for a few minutes when the mother finally snapped and grabbed hold of the older one and said, 'I have had enough of you misbehaving, now I am telling you this only once. You will hold onto this pram for the rest of the day, or otherwise, you will be in serious trouble when you get home, do you understand.'

I must admit I thought it was a bit harsh as she was putting the pram into the boot.

1953

Ruby Wax 1953 -

Ruby Wachs was born in Illinois in 1953 and later moved to Chicago with her family.

She is an American actress, comedian, lecturer and author. Wax has also made a name for herself as a mental health campaigner; she now lives in the UK.

Ruby was the daughter of Edward and Berthe Wachs. Her parents were Austrian Jews who fled Austria in 1938 because of the Nazi threat at the time. Edward was a sausage manufacturer, and her mother was an accountant.

Wax started a degree in psychology at the University of California in Berkeley, which she left after a year, Wax moved to the UK. In the UK, she studied at the Royal Scottish Academy of Music and Drama in Glasgow. She started her acting career at the Crucible Theatre in Sheffield, where she wrote and performed in a partnership with Alan Rickman.

She has performed in various roles, including the Royal Shakespeare Company and a TV credit on The Professionals. In 1981 she appeared in the film 'Shock Treatment' (a follow on from the 'Rocky Horror Picture Show') and 'Absolutely Fabulous'.

It was in 1985 that she got comedy recognition in the sitcom 'Girls on Top'. Following this, in 1987, Wax was given her own comedy chat show 'Don't Miss Wax' on Channel 4. Appearances on BBC 1 followed with 'The Full Wax' (1991-1994), and following that, she interviewed famous people on 'Ruby Wax meets...', which included Madonna, Imelda Marcos, OJ Simpson, Pamela Anderson and Sarah, Duchess of York. Wax has also worked with Comic Relief in various guises.

In 2010 and 2011, Wax produced her stand-up show 'Losing It', which focused on clinical depression, at the Duchess Theatre; it was because of the audiences' reactions that Ruby Wax founded a mental health website.

Ruby's Famous quotes:

'Exactly how old is Joan Collins? We need an expert. Someone who counts the rings on trees.'

'I've told so many lies about my age; I don't know how old I am myself.'

'My ultimate fantasy is to entice a man to my bedroom, put a gun to his head and say, 'make babies or die.'

'How come every other organ in your body can get sick, and you get sympathy, except the brain.'

'Being a mother is hard, and it wasn't a subject I ever studied.'

Ruby talked about organs. So, I have added an old Jewish joke on the subject:

A Jewish man went into hospital to have a tonsillectomy. He was very nervous, and the nurse could see this; he was having problems filling out the admissions form. 'Don't worry, this medical condition is easily fixed, and it's not a dangerous procedure,' she said.

The man looks at her and says, 'Yes, I know, I'm being a bit silly, go on, carry on with the questions, please.'

'Good.' Said the nurse. 'Now, do you have a living will?'

Henry Churniavsky's insight *into being a mother.*

Ten signs that I'm becoming a Jewish Mother:

It's only now, as I come out of my mid-life crisis and with my mother still with us, that I see there are early signs that I am becoming a male Jewish mother/grandmother!

1. I say things like, 'It's fine, don't worry about me.' I am shocked when people believe me…I'm now using lines my mum says and my grandma said in everyday life.
2. When a friend does not text you after a crazy night out, I now assume that he or she is dead!

Why else does the friend ignore six texts and voicemails?

3. *I'm at an age now when I leave the house, I take a sweater, and I look at people, out on a night out who aren't dressed warm enough (especially Liverpool girls), and I ask myself...do they want to get pneumonia and die?*
4. *Now an umbrella is part of me on a night out! Like my mum used to say, 'If you don't take one, it will rain...remember Noah and the ark.'*
5. *I now assume any minor injury is potentially fatal.*
6. *I am also now convinced I will die in an obscure accident. I spend time making sure I prevent this. I won't go near a building site at night and won't mow the lawn. Did you know several people die each year from dodgy lawn mowers? I remember, in my early 30s, I borrowed a hover mover, and I only used it once because I cut across the lead...it was a miracle I was not electrocuted - I learnt a valuable lesson that day.*
7. *I've developed selective hearing – sorry, what did you say?*
8. *My mother-in-law, Gd bless her, instilled into my wife and now me to never, ever go anywhere without a snack on you. Did you know it's medically proven by Jewish mothers that it only takes two hours for blood pressure to drop? And*

four hours to get dizzy and with only five hours, without food you can pass out.
9. On the subject of food, don't let food go to waste. My MIL insisted that seconds at a dinner table was never enough, thirds for every course. Hey, look at me! Do I look like a man who lets food go to waste?
10. You tell your children, marry for love, but whoever you do fall in love with, they had better be Jewish. This is what my grandmother always told me growing up. My grandfather always poo-pooed this idea 'Hey, don't listen to her, don't do what I did, marry someone with gelt (money); I tell you it's easier! They were happily married for over 60 years.

Rita Rudner 1953 –

Rudner was born in Miami, Florida, in 1953. An American comedian, she started as a Broadway dancer but noticed a lack of female comedians in New York, so she turned to stand-up, where she has been for over 30 years, becoming one of the major stars in the 1980s.

Rita was the daughter of Frances, a homemaker and Abe Rudner, a lawyer. Rudner lost her mum when she was only 13. After graduating from high school, she decided to go to New York and be a dancer. Appearing in several Broadway shows, including 'Follies' (1971) and 'Mack & Mabel' (1974), she then took a role in 'Annie' in 1979, only to leave in 1981.

At 25, Rudner turned to comedy; her idols were Woody Allen and Jack Benny. Her Jewish humour she would keep for a Jewish audience. The 1970s saw Rudner start her career, and in 1982 she made her debut on 'Late Night with David Letterman'. Television shows followed, not just in America but in the UK. She appeared on 'The Tonight Show Starring Johnny Carson' many times. Her epigrammatic style won many admirers in the early 1980s.

Her first solo show, 'Rita Rudner One Night Stand', was nominated for several awards. She recorded several other award-winning comedy specials, which included 'Rita Rudner: Born to be Mild' and 'Rita Rudner: Married

Without Children', then in 2008 'Rita Rudner: Live From Las Vegas'. Rudner was now performing all over the country; sell-out shows at Carnegie Hall (three times) and the Universal Amphitheatre (twice). She has also performed in Australia and England.

1992 saw Rita and her husband write the screenplay for 'Peter's Friends' in which she acted; it was a film that starred Emma Thompson, Hugh Laurie, Stephen Fry, Imelda Staunton and Kenneth Branagh (who won the Peter Seller's award for best comedy film). Another script from the duo 'a Weekend in the Country' with Jack Lemmon, Dudley Moore, Rita and Richard Lewis. Rudner also appeared in the 2011 film 'Thanks'.

Rudner has also written several books, 'I Still Have It: I Just Can't Remember Where I Left It.', 'Naked Beneath My Clothes', and a number of novels.

Since 2000 Rudner has performed, mainly in Las Vegas. She has become the longest solo comedy show in Las Vegas, performing at The Venetian since 2011.

Rudner has also created and hosted an improv comedy show 'Ask Rita' for which she received a Gracie Allen Award.

Rita's Famous quotes:

'I don't plan to grow old gracefully. I plan to have face-lifts until my ears meet.'

'My husband gave me a necklace. It's fake. I requested a fake. I'm paranoid, but in this day and age, I don't want something around my neck that's worth more than my head.'

'My husband and I have decided to start a family while my parents are still young enough to look after them.'

'My grandmother was a very tough woman. She buried three husbands. Two of them were just napping.'

'I love being married. It's so great to find that one special person you want to annoy for the rest of your life.'

'I think men who have a pierced ear are better prepared for marriage. They've experienced pain and brought jewellery.'

'My husband and I are either going to buy a dog or have a child. We can't decide whether to ruin our carpet or ruin our lives.'

'Some people think having large breasts makes a woman stupid. Actually, it's quite the opposite; a woman having large breasts makes men stupid.'

'The word 'aerobics' came about when the gym instructors got together and said if we're going to charge $10 an hour, we can't call it jumping up and down.'

'Male menopause is a lot more fun than female menopause; with female menopause, you gain weight and get hot flushes. Male menopause...you get to date young girls and drive motorcycles.'

Rita talked about marriage in her act. So, I have added an old Jewish joke on the subject:

A daughter comes home from an afternoon out with her boyfriend, Alex, who looks very unhappy. Her mum says, 'What's the matter, darling?'
'Alex has asked me to marry him.'
"That's amazing, Mazeltov, but why are you looking so sad?'
My daughter says, 'Because he has just told me he is an atheist. Oh, Mum, he doesn't even believe in hell.'
'Don't worry; it's not really a problem. I suggest you marry him, and between the two of us, we'll show him how wrong he is.'

Henry Churniavsky's insight *into menopause.*

My wife went through menopause; it was not fun for her or me. Those mood swings - I've still got them!

Luckily there was a new medical product on the market to help with the hot flushes. It was called Ladycare, known as 'The Menopause Magnet'. This was a magnet that a woman would place on the front of her underwear. It works, I assure you, but it did have some side effects; for instance, every time my wife walked past the fridge, her pelvis would stick to the door. On the plus side, she could open the dishwasher with one thrust. Eating in restaurants did, however, come at a price. As soon as she sat down, you could see the cutlery moving off the table towards her groin area. On the plus side, we now have a new fabulous set in our dining room.

Being a hypochondriac, I did check out the leaflet for any side effects, and one was it could improve your libido, so I've ordered another set for me!

Men suffer menopause too, you know. Like it says on the tin - men on pause.

1954

Jerry Seinfeld 1954 -

Seinfeld was born in New York City in 1954. He is an American comedian, actor, writer, producer and director. He is best known for his work with Larry David on 'Seinfeld'.

Jerry's father, Kalman, was of Hungarian descent, and he collected jokes he had heard while serving in the army. His mother was Betty. Her parents were from Syria.

Seinfeld attended the Massapequa High School on Long Island and, at 16, went to live on a Kibbutz in Israel. On returning to the States, he graduated from the State University of New York at Oswego in communications and theatre.

Seinfeld had several jobs before getting his big break. He sold jewellery from a cart and even worked as a light-bulb salesman *(but he saw the light eventually - sorry!).* Seinfeld's comedy career started in stand-up after doing open mics at some of his college productions at Budd Friedman's Improv Club while at college. In 1976 he did an open mic in New York at Catch a Rising Star, which led him to appear on Rodney Dangerfield's HBO special. He also had a short stint in the sitcom 'Benson' in 1980.

In 1981 saw Seinfeld appeared on 'The Tonight Show Starring Johnny Carson' and 'Late Night with David Lederman', amongst others.

In 1987 he had his first one-hour special, 'Stand-Up Confidential' on HBO and 1988–1998 saw the TV show 'Seinfeld' become the most-watched sitcom on American TV. After the end of 'Seinfeld', Jerry returned to New York, from Los Angeles, and continue with stand-up. He toured in 1998 for 'I'm Telling You for the Last Time'.

In 2008 he had a special one-off, one-night-only tour at the Hammerstein Ballroom for the 'Stand Up for a Cure' charity in aid of lung cancer. Then in 2011, another tour brought him to England for the first time in 11 years. In 2012 Seinfeld started 'Comedians in Cars Getting Coffee', where he would pick up a comedian and go for coffee (*easy, really!*). Amongst the guests have been Dave Chappelle, Eddie Murphy, Louis CK, Mel Brooks, Don Rickles, Jerry Lewis, Ellen DeGeneres and others.

In 2014 Seinfeld hosted a special with Don Rickles: 'One Night Only at the Apollo Theatre'. In 2017 while still working and making TV appearances, he performed in the stand-up comedy special 'Jerry Before Seinfeld'.

Jerry has also produced comedy albums, 'I'm Telling You for the Last Time' (1998), and 'Jerry Before Seinfeld' (2017).

Jerry's Famous quotes:

'Sometimes the road less travelled is less travelled for a reason.'

'I am so busy doing nothing...that the idea of doing anything - which as you know, always leads to something - cuts into the nothing and then forces me to have to drop everything.'

'Now they show you how detergents take out bloodstains – a pretty violent image there. I think if you've got a T-shirt with a bloodstain all over it, maybe laundry isn't your biggest problem. Maybe you should get rid of the body before you do the wash.'

'It's amazing that the amount of news that happens in the world every day always just exactly fits the newspaper.'

'A bookstore is one of the only pieces of evidence we have that people are still thinking.'

'What is the age people reach when they decide, when they back out of the driveway, there're not looking anymore? You know how they do that? They just go, 'Well. I'm old, and I'm backing out. I survived; let's see if you can.''

'No matter how much time you save, at the end of your life, there's no extra time saved up. You'll be going.'

'What do you mean there's no time? I had a microwave oven, Velcro sneakers, a clip-on tie. Where's the time? But there isn't any. Because when you waste time in life, they subtract it. Like if you saw all the Rocky movies, they deduct that.'

'Make no mistake about why babies are here. They're here to replace us.'

'My parents didn't want to move to Florida, but they turned 60, and that's the law.'

Henry Churniavsky's insight *into getting older (turned 60) and new text abbreviations.*

LOL – Living on laxative
FML – Fucked my liver
PMP - Pissed my pants
HGBM – Had good bowel movement
DTAF – Don't trust a fart
PHD – prostate has doubled
GHA – Got heartburn again
ATDA – At the Dr's again
INE – I need an enema
DWI – Driving while incontinent
PIMP – got called a PIMP the other day, Pooped my pants.
FWIW – Forget where I am
Jewish text – JK – Just kvetching

Henry Churniavsky's insight *into babies:*

Just over 30 years ago, my wife and I had twins.

As a side issue, before I talk about my twins, on children and pregnancy, I was recently walking past a maternity ward (I work in hospitals, so it's not strange. I do not just hang around maternity wards for a laugh). I noticed a pregnancy leaflet – a help guide with questions from the public. These were not available in our day. No real books to speak of; you just got on with it. I was intrigued and read the questions and answers. I've listed below some of the questions apparently asked, but as a Jewish father of twins, I have changed the answers to what I think the answers should be. And I have updated them for today's parents to be

1. *I am pregnant; what do I need to do next? My answer today - I would suggest you find a husband if you can.*
2. *I'm two months pregnant now, when will the baby move? The answer today would be – with a bit of luck if they get a job a few years after completing university. If no job, never.*
3. *What is the most reliable method to determine the sex of the baby? The answer, childbirth!*
4. *My wife is five months pregnant and is so moody that sometimes she's borderline irrational – sorry, so what is the question?*

5. This is a technical question. When is the foetus viable? From a Jewish perspective, it's when he or she graduates from university
6. When is the best time for an epidural? Good question this one (I asked the wife). Right after you find out you are pregnant.
7. Should I have a baby after 35? – No, definitely not; 35 children are more than enough!
8. My childbirth instructor says it's not pain you feel during birth, but pressure, is he right? Over to you, my dear wife, for your answer to this question. Answer - ask him is it PRESSURE he feels when I hope he feels like he's passed a large kidney stone through his penis. (I think that answered the question, don't you?).
9. Now a question which must be from the man. Is there a reason I have to be in the delivery room while my wife is in labour? – No, not at all, as long as you want to have your testicles removed without anaesthetic.
10. And finally, I think this is a question you decide. Our baby was born last week. When will my wife begin to feel and act normal again? I could not possibly comment.

Jerry was also a massive fan of Abbott and Costello and once said, 'If it weren't for Abbott and Costello, many of the wonderful burlesque routines which are a part of *the American fabric would have been lost forever. They were giants of their time who truly immortalised burlesque forever. Maybe that art form is largely lost, but I try and keep it alive in my own show.'*

Chapter 6 - Tips for Stand-up Comedians

(For those who might want to try!)

So, you want to give it a go. Are you sure? I can, with hand on heart, say, I love the business of stand-up. It's not for everyone, but I do believe everyone has a funny story to tell, and you should try it.

Are you the person who has been told, 'Hey, that was funny; you should be on the stage!' Or when you were just chatting away, have people said you should give stand-up a go? Have you got ideas in your brain which you are dying to do something with?

Well, maybe stand-up is for you. Hey, it costs nothing; you've got nothing to lose – well, except your dignity, morale and self-confidence. Only joking!

Comedy is about enjoying making others laugh. As I have said, we all have something funny that has happened to us or we have seen. We have all seen professional comedians on the TV or on stage, and I bet you think they must just come up with this while they are performing; it seems so natural to them. That's the art of it, to make it look like its natural. But I can assure you every comedian will work on an idea, write about it, perform it, change it, re-write it many, many times and then try it on different audiences. No two audiences are the same, I can assure you.

*I remember my first Edinburgh Fringe Festival. I went up only to jump on some shows and do five or, if lucky, ten minutes. I was very lucky as I met a great comedian **Masai Graham**, who let me do my shtick at a number of events around Edinburgh. At one particular gig, while I was up there, Masai had five comics, all doing five minutes and a closing act doing fifteen, and he was the MC. We had the same line-up for three days: same comics, same material, same everything. The only difference was the audience.*

On day one, we all had a blast, and all did well. The second day Masai was starting his MC bit, and the audience was not as easy as the previous day. Masai continued and then introduced the first act. He came off and said to me, 'This is a tough crowd today; I think we will all suffer.' He was right; we all had a hard time with the same stuff from the previous day. On day three, we tried again, a different audience. And while Masai was delivering the same killer lines as the day before to silence, the laughs started to roar, and then the first act went, and he had the same, followed by myself - and the following acts all killed their sets. So, remember it is not always you the comic. Ok, back to tips.

To start with a set, you can look at yourself and find something funny in you and develop this either as part of the act or part of your style. You need a three to five-minute routine to get you started. It can be a joke with a beginning, middle and an end (called a segue); it can also be a two-part joke with a 'set up' and 'the punch line'.

The most important part of a joke is to start to practice, practice and practice. Start at home, maybe even record it and listen to it a few times.

Stand in front of a mirror, get comfortable; people will be looking at you, so get used to it early on! You need to look relaxed, despite the fact you may be, and I apologise for the term, 'shitting a brick'. Perform your set in front of a few people you know, ask them what they liked, try and get different types of people and see how they react. Don't just get friends who will laugh at anything you say; I don't think this will help in the long run.

It's not comfortable doing it in front of people you know, but if you can, that's real pressure! Do this, and an unknown audience is easier in some ways. When you start, it may not be easy at the beginning, but I find performing comedy to people I know is harder at times.

Once you have a script, get it recorded or, even better, videoed. It's a great way to learn. Watch it back, yes; it's hard to watch yourself, but it is worth the pain! See where the laughs are, see where the laughs don't come, but don't be put off as I have already alluded to no two crowds are the same.

With regards to your material, make sure its unique to you. Don't watch other comics and do their material. In this field, using others' material is not a form of flattery (as the saying goes). This does not mean you can't use some ideas. But, hey, be yourself, look at funny situations you find yourself in. Listen to people who are around; they can be a great inspiration.

Recently (I have added this joke into this book, but it is based on a true story with only the ending changed to make it funnier – well, I think so, and it makes the point), I was in Liverpool city centre; I was off to meet a comedian who I had been in contact with, and he was gigging that night in the city.
While I was walking, I noticed a harassed young mum with two kids. She was pushing the buggy which carried the youngest child in, and an elder child, aged around three or four, walking beside the buggy. Suddenly he walked away, and his mother screamed at him to come back to her. But a few seconds later, he was off again. The mother stopped and shouted again. She said, "Get here right now; I am losing my patience with you. Now you are to have one hand on this buggy for the rest of the day, and if you don't, you will be in serious trouble when you get home. Do you understand me?"
The boy looked sheepishly and said yes and apologised again, and he held the buggy while they carried on into town. Now while this is not a joke in itself, it was the start of a possible joke (you may even think it is not one at the end, but that's your prerogative!). So, I made a note of the event. When I got home, I read the note, and I added the lines - now you are to have one hand on this buggy for the rest of the day. I must admit I thought it was a bit harsh of the mother as she was

actually putting the buggy in the boot of her car at the time!

OK, maybe not that funny, I liked it, and I have tried it out and got a few laughs, but I think you get the gist.

Ok, you're ready. Learn as much as you can of your 3-5 minutes. Some comics at the start of their career or even comics who have been around for a long time write notes on their hand. I use a card occasionally on a table in case I lose my way. And at my age, that's a lot!

The next thing to do is get a gig under your belt. An open spot they are called. Facebook is a great tool for this. Get to know the manager of the place, introduce yourself and tell them you are new, speak to the other comics and get their input on the place, and ask about other gigs that you could try and get on to.

*I was lucky I went on a comedy course, and I highly recommend this. After the course, we did a gig at the Empire Theatre with all the new people from the course and with a couple of comics from a previous year. We all invited our family and friends, and it was an amazing night. A thank you to **Sam Avery**, who masterminded the course, and another shout out to **John Wilson**, who had done a previous course who came to help. He was the one (you can all blame) who got me to come to his gig and carry on being a stand-up comedian.*

Ok, back to the gig. It is important for you to watch how the MC and the comedians who are on before you use the microphone. At what distance are they getting the best sound? If you get a chance before the gig starts, try it out. You want to make sure, now that you have taken the plunge, that you can be heard. Also, make sure you know the timings of your routine. Sometimes the MC will flash a light which will mean there's one minute left (check with them before, so you know). Some comedians wear a watch with a timer. So just be aware about timings, that's all in the early days.

So now the first gig is done. Good or bad, you have done it, so do it again, soon. Listen back to the set. Learn from it. Rewrite some of it and try that out next time. There will be a next time. Be critical of your work, rewrite or get rid and replace. Maybe even work in collaboration with some other comics. Ask, you never know, and hey, two or three brains are better than one. It has helped me; sometimes, another person has a line they will give you, which is better. Thank them; you may be able to help them as well.

With regards to doing stand-up comedy, a comedian needs stage time. Like an athlete, they train and train more to be the best they can be. So, do as much as possible to be the best you can be. All my comedy friends advised me when I started, a while ago, that I should just get out there and enjoy. Practice is what is needed; it's stage time you need, not just rehearsing in front of a mirror. Stage time is THE most important thing. It helps with your timing of the jokes, your breathing; you learn when to pause more effectively and when to stop and start. But this takes time. It will get to a point you will feel natural on the stage. Yes, you will always be nervous, that's fine, but the more you do, the better most comedians become.

As I said in one of my quotes, crowds can be different; not all audiences laugh out loud, but they can be a good audience; it just needs you to work through it. I always record my sets and listen back. It's very useful to hear back and listen to yourself and the crowd.

Remember everyone has a bad night; even the best have bombed in their time, more than once! It is one of those awful feelings, that deadly silence. If you don't pass out or break into a sweat, all you need is a deep breath and move on. That's the best thing to do.

Hecklers: Hopefully, especially at the start of your time as a comedian, you won't get heckled. A good MC will ask the audience not to heckle the comedians, and in the main, they don't. However, it can happen, be prepared. Remember, not everyone will find you funny, and 99% of people won't say anything. If someone shouts out something, you can do one of several things. First, you can ignore and just carry on, probably the best thing to do early on in a career. Next, you can respond. Be dismissive or make a joke about it, but don't insult; that's the worst thing to do. Try and think of a reply and keep it in your memory.

I remember once getting heckled at a gig in Blackpool. I must have read this come-back somewhere; I really don't remember (I later saw this anonymous quote in a put-down book). I was talking about gluttony, and ok, I am not slim. I will say that. This woman shouted, 'Yes, I can see that.' My first reaction was to look for what I assumed would be a skinny woman shouting this, but no, it was a very large woman, and I could have been a bit nasty, but I came back with 'Ladies and gentlemen some comedians have plants in the audience, what do I get ...a vegetable.' The crowd laughed, and I continued with the set. Later, during the break, the woman in question came up to me to apologise and thanked me for not being horrible to her; she said she did not know why she blurted it out (probably the alcohol consumed made her feel brave) and then said she enjoyed my set.

One very weird heckle came from a gentleman who was not even in the room; in fact, he was not even in the building. Puzzled? Let me explain. I was doing a summer gig in a suburb of Liverpool, and it was a hot night. The room was busy, and the door to the outside area for drinking and smoking was open to let some air in. I had just started my routine, and I heard 'Shut the F**k up.' The MC stood up and looked at the audience, and I was looking for the heckler; no one could be identified. The MC even went outside, and no one was in the courtyard;

he came back and, while I was continuing, looked at me and shrugged as he had no idea. Two minutes later, 'I told you to shut the f**k up' - laughter ensued in the audience, and we could tell it was from outside, so the MC went out again and came back laughing. He said, 'It's ok, it's some bloke in a house with the window open backing onto the courtyard... I told him f**k off back.' Well, that got the best response to my set. Yep heckled by someone not even in the building - beat that!

There have been some great quotes from comedians with regards to hecklers, and here are a few I enjoyed reading.

Heckler: 'What do you do for a living?'
Rodney Dangerfield: 'I get guys for your sister.'
And another come back from the great man, 'Hey buddy, you ought to save your breath. You'll need it later to blow up your inflatable date.'

Some other anonymous quotes:
'If my dog had a face like yours, I'd shave its arse and teach it to walk backwards.'

'When god put teeth in your mouth, he ruined a perfectly good arsehole.' *I see a pattern emerging here.*

One of the best I read was from the great Bob Monkhouse. I once had the pleasure of seeing him perform live at a nightclub in Liverpool, and he was amazing. He asked audiences for topics, and he had a joke for them all. He did nearly two hours.

Monkhouse: 'Madam, do you make that much noise when you're making love?'
Female heckler: 'No.'
Monkhouse: 'Well, would someone please come and f**k her.'

I don't want to finish this book on a negative, i.e. a heckler. What I will end on is this. Doing stand-up comedy has opened a new world for me. I have met some amazing comedians on the way *(some arseholes as well, but a small minority)*. Most comedians are great people. Doing stand-up has given me more confidence, and I just love it when I hear people laugh at stuff I say. The best part is when someone from the audience takes time to come and speak to you after your set and say "thank you" or "I enjoyed your set" or "your joke on..." THAT IS WHAT IT IS ALL ABOUT.

So, if you think you have a joke or two to go on, give it a go. Make that next step - it's amazing

Thank you for reading, and I hope you found some enjoyment from my book.

Henry

All profits from sales are being given to Laugh For Life Charity. Thank you.

Acknowledgements & Source Material

Encyclopaedia Britannica
Spotify
Wikipedia
Brainy Quote
Kings of Comedy – Acton & Webb
Wayback Machine
IMDd.com
Harry Steins 'Esquire Magazine' June 1976
The Big Book Of Wrinklies' Wit and Wisdom – Jarski, Rattle & Vale
Jewish Comedy a Serious History – Jeremy Dawber
Kliph Nesteroff: Interviews
A Yiddish Guide to Jack Carter – M. Wolfe
The Joys of Yiddish – Leo Rosten
The Official Marty Feldman Website
The Borscht Belt – Adams & Tobias
Seriously Funny – The Rebel Comedians of the 1950s & 60s – Gerald Nachman